FINANCIAL

HELPING FINANCIAL SERVICES EXECUTIVES PREPARE FOR AN ARTIFICIAL WORLD

KIRK DRAKE

Financial

Helping Financial Services Executives Prepare for an Artificial World

ISBN   978-1-7344078-0-8 *Hardcover*

   978-1-7344078-1-5 *Paperback*

   978-1-7344078-2-2 *Ebook*

Thanks to my wonderful wife, who has been supportive of all the crazy ups and downs and distractions of entrepreneurship.

FORWARD

by John Best

One question I am constantly asked by financial institutions is: "What areas of our business will AI impact?"

The answer is simple: everything.

The author of is the book is someone I have worked with for many years and someone that I greatly respect. Especially his visions and leadership in our industry. Mr. Drake and I speak often, usually to compare notes and breakthroughs we see in technology. We both closely watch the big players like Google, apple, amazon, and Facebook. We both realized there was an emerging theme to our conversations: Artificial Intelligence.

As we discussed the market and the problems that our clients and friends in the industry face, we like to kick around creative solutions using the technology we both have seen and have been experimenting with.

As it turns out, the game changer was data + AI.

Growth Problems? Use external data and AI to find new members.

Loans? Use data and AI to make better loans and provide better rates to your most worthy members.

Service? Data + AI will allow your organization become prescriptive to provide financial advice, predict the members next need.

Deposits? AI will allow you to better predict your cash flow. As well as provide information on how to drive behavior.

Branches or kiosks? Let AI and data inform your business strategy.

The power of AI cannot be understated. Its importance to your future also cannot be understated.

Read on to learn from a true visionary. You will learn what it can do, how you can do it, and who will need, and where to put them, the future of your organization depends on how well your group implements AI.

PREFACE

How To Read This Book

This book took longer to write than I expected. For
one, writing a book is hard when there's so much else
to do. But really, the subject matter itself was a constant battle. I cannot overstate this enough.

The technologies at play in Financial are progressing rapidly. By the time I had finished my first draft, several salient new examples of AI had emerged, and I included them in my first revision. By then, most of the organizations I highlighted in my case studies had increased their efficiency considerably. (This is a common theme in AI solutions.)

At some point, however, one must actually publish—no matter how quickly the subject matter progresses. And so here we are.

The purpose of this book is threefold. First, it will provide a background on AI—both inside and outside the financial industry. Second, it will show how AI is being used in banks and credit unions. Finally, it will outline the steps you'll need to take (and the resources required) to begin using AI in your financial institution.

If you're not very familiar with AI already, I recommend starting at the very beginning. It's a short read, and it contextualizes a lot of what you'll read in the second and third sections. It may also give you and idea of the brief history of AI, how far it's come in such a short time, and how quickly it will grow from here.

If you're comfortable with your understanding of AI but you're not convinced that it has many real-world applications—especially in your industry—then you can probably skip right to the second section. In it, I illustrate how widespread and advanced this technology is already. Yes, even in institutions like yours!

Finally, if you want to begin working with AI immediately, go ahead and start with the third section. This is the action-oriented portion of the book, and it will help you plan for your own foray into the world of AI. Essentially, it's a loose playbook filled with strategies, recommendations, and considerations for implementing AI solutions at your institution.

The most important thing I want to communicate is urgency. I hope it's fun. I hope it's informative. But above all, I hope it inspires you to do something— and soon.

CONTENTS

SECTION 1: A PRIMER ON AI

SECTION 2: REAL-WORLD AI

SECTION 3: THE AI PLAYBOOK

PROLOGUE

___

When I was 16, I started a high school bank. The bank put me through two weeks of teller training and taught me about the evil industry: credit unions.

It was an interesting time in banking. ATMs were just going mainstream and the bank just got its first computer in the branch—a fancy addition, to be sure. I was doing batch deposits using offline procedures, cashing paychecks, and earning free key chains and beach towels in return for training customers to use an ATM. Things were great.

At the same time, we were at the beginning of a crazy trend in massive digital change coming to the financial services space. The future came quickly, featuring the PC revolution, client servers, the internet, online and mobile banking, mobile wallets, and data analytics—each advancement made us more efficient, more dependent on technology, and slowly morphed us into technology companies without us even knowing it.

Sure, there were small indicators that our roles were shifting along the way. For example, I distinctly remember the fight to be renamed from Data Processing to Information Technology. In credit union IT departments, we used to spend 99% of our time on operations and reports. Now, that workload is almost entirely automated. Nevertheless, we have 10 times the number of IT people we used to. But most changes, regardless of how gradual, subtle, or behind-the-scenes they felt, were building momentum toward our modern technological landscape.

I've been a serial entrepreneur for most of my life. My desire to breathe new life into old ideas—or to see my plans come to fruition—has propelled me toward the cutting edge of financial technologies. Although the entrepreneurial spirit is in my blood, there's a hint of stubbornness there, too. If some of the ideas or technologies in this book sound outlandish to you, well, I can relate.

See, my grandfather was a talented entrepreneur. Willis Kirk Drake helped start Control Data Corporation and DataCard. When I visited him as a kid, he had about 25 Betamax machines setup to record TV shows for collecting. VHS came out shortly thereafter and was clearly dominating the market. Grandpa was about 75 when all this was going on. I asked him when he would convert the Betamax tapes to VHS. His response was priceless. He said, "Kirk, I have maybe 10–15 years left on this planet. I own 25 Betamax machines and I have 10 more in box. I am not going to convert. It's not worth it."

I thought it was funny then, but seeing the same behavior from some banks and credit unions now is just frustrating. Maybe they think their stockpiles of slightly outdated technology will last them another decade. Maybe they're worried that an investment for the future won't pay off in the short term. Maybe they're near retirement and have stopped planning ahead. Or, maybe they're just putting their heads in the sand so they don't have to confront reality. But it's frustrating, because the right thing for them to do is to set their institutions down a path with higher potential for their investors, members, and employees.

I don't want to describe a problem without identifying any solutions, though. Time and again, when I speak with financial institutions about the technology they use and what they expect to see on the horizon, I realize that many people in the financial industry haven't kept in touch with what's happening in the digital realm. They aren't aware that there are companies with solutions out there who are willing to partner with or compete against financial institutions. Many in our industry aren't even aware that some of these technologies exist, to say nothing of the fact that we must either incorporate or compete with these technologies to survive.

With that in mind, I want to take some time to introduce you to a few of the more common technologies that feature prominently in the financial sector. For that purpose, I've gone back to my roots and played around with the development side of things. I'd like to introduce JPEG, the Offline Heuristic Nanobot:

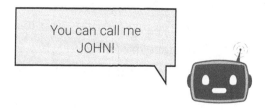

JOHN is the *best* robot friend anyone could ask for. He'll pop up sometimes to explain complicated technical terms, emerging technologies, and other tools of the AI trade. Don't worry, though: JOHN won't get too technical. He knows that this isn't that kind of book. He's just here to translate jargon into something the rest of us can easily understand.

Looking Towards the Future

With all of this already in the past, you might think that the pace of change will slow down. It won't. In fact, that pace is going to increase. A lot. Artificial Intelligence and machine learning are about to unleash a wave of change that will make the past 25 years seem slow.

Financial institutions don't always innovate at the same speed as other industries. In my experience, the pace of change in an organization is directly related to that of the slowest person. Usually, this "slowest person" has been there a long time, has lots of institutional knowledge, and is often a favorite among staff. However, this same person requires constant retraining, and they're just counting down the years (or months) to retirement. The challenge we're facing now is that this round of change won't allow for us to let Sally retire in three years at her pace. This change is going to be disruptive, swift, and painful. AI and machine learning have been in development for more than a half a century, and we are turning a major corner in its sophistication.

Some scientists are predicting that AI will take over all human jobs in the next 25 years. Others predict it will be 100 years. Either way, if anything close to that happens anywhere in that time frame, we are all going to see major change in our jobs, societies, and our financial institutions. Let's face it, humans are still the new players in this game. Dinosaurs had about 60 million years on the planet to evolve. Humans have had about 300,000+ years. We are really early in our evolutionary advancement. For most of human development, progress has been a nice consistent pace. But what if that were about to change? What if through our invention of computers, the internet, and now Artificial Intelligence, we create the catalyst for a huge explosion of knowledge, automation, and progress that makes our nice linear progression seem tame?

Sometimes, change occurs slowly. It occurs so slowly that it's hard to see it while it's happening. That's how human progress was for hundreds of thousands of years. However, in the world of AI and machine learning, the pace of evolution is accelerating. Soon, that pace may be exponential.

As I continued to work with forward-thinking financial institutions and fintechs, I started seeing some major trends. Some companies hadn't just embraced digital transformation—they were actively pushing the world in a tech-heavy direction. They were working with software that was the stuff of dreams since the world first started working on AI. They were ready to either partner with traditional financial institutions or displace them. Then again, I've seen many financial institutions struggle to adopt technologies that have been available—and even considered standard—for more than a decade, such as the cloud.

"Fintech" is short for financial technology. Companies that provide banking services or support for banking services are often called fintechs.

A few popular fintechs you may know include Venmo for peer-to-peer payments, Acorns for investing and basic checking, Ripple and Bitcoin in blockchain and cryptocurrency, and Square for payments processing.

RE: Fintechs

It certainly raises the question: if a financial institution isn't using the cloud, how are they going to prepare for machine learning and natural language processing? As I will demonstrate in this book, those AI technologies are already seeing mainstream success in the financial world. Such technology is poised to change the way our industry works.

There's an old saying that goes, "if you can't beat 'em, join 'em." I'm not confident that most financial institutions have what it takes to beat the most disruptive, innovative technology companies out there. Beating them might not be in the cards. On the other hand, there's no blueprint on how to "join 'em," either. With that in mind, I wanted to write a book that outlines the technologies in play: what to look for, what to expect, and possibly, just possibly, how to "join 'em."

Why do we care? What are we concerned about?

Over the past 25 years, I have watched financial institutions be consistently late adopters of technology trends. Often, financial institutions struggle with innovation or change, so they spend a lot of time playing catch-up.

New IT people in the industry are seriously disturbed at the gaps. However, while they push the boundaries in the first couple of years of their financial technology careers, it's not long before the industry gets the best of them. Whether regulation or core systems, legacy technology often holds banks and credit unions back, or it requires complicated workarounds and cumbersome technological band-aids. After a few board planning sessions and technology budgets, the general lack of enthusiasm for leading edge technology rears its ugly head.

And that's a problem. Fresh IT professionals begin worrying about typical industry technology issues, and they forget that the world of technology is miles ahead of the financial industry. Rather than revolutionize the system, they start looking for ways to work within it, accepting as immutable the limitations therein. They get assimilated, and then complacent—they miss trends, opportunities for gains in efficiency, and the drive for innovation.

In other industries, failure to accept change and innovation has had disastrous consequences. Digital music files and streaming services revolutionized the music industry. Online stores changed the face of retail as we know it. Currently, the ground shipping industry is dealing with the threat of self-driving trucks. It's critical that the financial industry doesn't follow the same path and let technology companies take over their market.

After spending many years striving for innovation, I came across a great model for looking at innovation road maps*. This model categorizes trends I have seen repeated within our industry. I've changed the model a little bit to fit what I see as the four phases of innovation in the IT and financial industries. One could argue that very few financial institutions move beyond the first phase.

Innovation Phase One
Minimal intrusion, short-term gains

In this phase, innovation means finding a way to perform some tasks more effectively or efficiently, which saves money over time. Phase One innovation ushers in improvements in cost savings, process efficiencies, and incremental revenues

For example, a financial institution might work with an AI-based loan origination platform. The

....

*   Imaginatik PLC

institution wouldn't change much about their business—or their approach to business—aside from relying more heavily on technology for some aspects of their loan portfolio.

This stage is like dipping one's toes into the waters of change. It's a start, but it's safe, noncommittal, and won't do much to get your ready to swim with the big fish.

Innovation Phase Two
Business-wide buy-in, tech-forward approach

In Phase Two, organizations welcome a digital-forward approach to new ideas. Innovation spurs developments in ideation volume, engagement levels, projects launched, HR-oriented measures, and functional metrics, which in turn capture board-level consideration.

For example, a financial institution might see how well the loan origination platform worked in Phase One. So, they decide to investigate other tech-based improvements. For example, they might integrate end-to-end workload automation to tie complex systems together. Or they could turn their card portfolio analytics project into an institution-wide appreciation for how analytics can fit into their greater goals.

This stage is more like wading in and getting a real feel for the current. You're waist deep, and you're actually starting to get a feel for what you're getting yourself into.

Innovation Phase Three
Cultural shift toward a digital-first strategy

Phase Three introduces a new approach to the way business is done. Innovation doesn't just play a small role—it extends forward to the customer experience, courts new technologies, and revolutionizes entire company ecosystems.

The biggest difference between Phase Two and Phase Three isn't with the technology they use. No, it's about how they approach, interact with, and integrate that technology. In Stage Three, businesses constantly reevaluate their tools and technology to ensure their ecosystem, processes, and procedures are digitally optimized.

In this stage, they're not just testing the waters— they're thriving in them.

Innovation Phase Four
Full metamorphosis, driver of innovation

The final phase of innovation is the largest and most transformational. At this stage, companies begin trend scouting, incubating new ideas, co-creating necessary technologies, scaling up, and otherwise fomenting or facilitating broader trends in the marketplace.

If Phase One is using a new technology, Phase Two is leveraging technology on multiple fronts, and Phase Three is creating a culture of innovation and technological optimization, then what is Phase Four? In the first three phases, companies follow trends. In Phase Four, companies create trends. They develop their own solutions and technologies to address institutional or industry-wide issues. Often, they're in uncharted territories.

No longer content with merely testing the waters, companies in Phase Four are like scuba divers: comfortable within their new landscape and ready to make discoveries.

The four phases of innovation are particularly interesting when you consider where financial institutions are situated in the market today—and where new companies are entering it. What does the start of your digital innovation look like? And how does your starting point affect your road map going forward?

Most smaller financial institutions reach Phase One every so often. Tools like ATMs, computers, and internet banking were once new. And each financial institution now embraces those tools because they're industry standards. Yet many smaller institutions were late adopters to these now-ubiquitous tools. They followed trends only after those trends had already begin revolutionizing the marketplace.

It's okay to start at Phase One (or even before it)! But just remember that the fintechs and major banks you're competing with aren't just following trends— they're also creating them. Some in our industry are starting with vulnerable, on-premise networks. Their road maps include items like migrating to the cloud, finding mobile banking apps, and leveraging analytics. Fintechs entering the scene stand in sharp contrast, though. They're cloud-based, they've got the app, and analytics already informs their every decision. Technologically speaking, they're years or even decades ahead. Instead of starting at or before Phase One, they're already in Phase Three or Four.

Ask yourself if your financial institution is truly ready to compete with the efficiency and convenience of new technologies. And before you answer, remember that at least for now:

You have more experience

You serve more people

Your approach is proven

Those considerations should give you a fighting chance, but only if you're willing to take new technology seriously. Otherwise, fintechs and major banks will do to our industry what Uber and Lyft did to taxis.

Innovation is (and should be) a major driving force in our changing financial landscape. Products of innovation empowers consumers, improves operational efficiency, and so much more. So, why are many smaller financial institutions so wary of it? I know we in this industry are particularly risk-averse, but surely we can see that some risks are warranted.

Almost every credit union, bank, and fintech starts with the understanding that they can provide better, faster, more convenient services *somehow*. They realize that technology exists that could help them save on costs while improving their products, services, or efficiency. They aim to reach Phase One, knowing that it's an easy win—the low hanging fruit on the path toward transformation and renewed relevance. They also believe that working together is key, and they muster the will to buckle down and achieve their new goal for improvement.

Then, it ends.

But it shouldn't stop there. Phase One is an easy target that saves money and reduces inefficiencies, but that's about the limit to those benefits. Continuing to the next phases brings far more potential. Plus, in industries that are threatened by more tech-savvy and innovative upstarts, it doesn't change the reality of the situation: when faced with the prospect of being overtaken by new approaches, failing to move beyond Phase One says two things.

First, halting innovation at Phase One says, "we understand that there may be newer, better ways of doing things, but we believe that we can compete by slightly improving the old way." Judging by the protracted decline of many brick-and-mortar establishments, it's not a safe bet to assume that minor improvements to the old ways have any long-term feasibility. But don't take my word for it—just ask Blockbuster how they feel about Netflix, or ask Sears if they think Amazon will be an existential threat.

Second, ceasing innovation after achieving Phase One tells people that a business doesn't prioritize evolution and improvement. It sends the message that competitors will always introduce the newest, latest, most useful, and most convenient products and services first. While consistency may be nice—nobody would have to worry about converting their Betamax tapes over to VHS, for example—it also means that they'll be dealing with consistently outdated approaches that cater to only the slowest adopters of change. While the rest of us are watching streaming content in 4k, they're just picking up DVDs and widescreen. Essentially, failing to push past Phase One of innovation indicates that a company is more concerned with maintaining a status quo than in delivering the best available product.

With AI, each phase of innovation is wide open to financial institutions. Other companies have already begun their journeys. Most have reached Phase One at this point. Many are flirting with Phases Two and Three. Researchers, fintechs, and other digital-first companies are creating a stir in Phase Four.

We're currently watching in real time as the world begins to adopt AI technologies. This is the period in which the groundwork for the future is being laid. If you run a business, think about what you want your business's future to look like. Consider what might happen if you put all your eggs in the Betamax basket even after VHS hit the scene. Hindsight may be 20/20, but history repeats itself. Think about which decisions you would have been proud of making in the past.

For example, imagine you could go back in time a decade before the dotcom era knowing what you know now. How would you invest your time and money? How would you operate a business back then? Would you be an early adopter of web technology? Or would you try to save resources by sticking with what you already know and are comfortable with, waiting for others to vet (and profit off of) the efficacy and long-term impact of the early internet?

Or, if you could go back to the beginning of the industrial revolution, would you continue doing business as usual? Or would you try to capitalize on your industry's newfound capacity to scale up? If you didn't embrace mechanization, you'd be stuck trying to do things by hand while others quickly surpassed your production abilities and undercut your prices. However, if you jumped on mechanization early, you could be a successful innovator.

Now, think about where you are in history now. You're anywhere from a few years to a decade out from the next version of the dotcom era or industrial revolution. AI and machine learning are the new stages of technology set to disrupt and redefine your industry. So, if you missed out on the opportunities of the previous technological eras, ask yourself: are you ready to miss out on AI?

From our childhoods, to our way of life, to the working world, almost every institution and experience is going to be impacted by the rise of AI. I argue that we shouldn't ignore it. We shouldn't wait until others have mastered and profited off the technology before we start paying attention. I argue that we should jump on the trend. We should learn, innovate, and leverage this next wave of technology to create great opportunities for our organizations.

Yes, working with AI might be a little risky. You could invest money in development that doesn't pan out well. You might put time and energy into working with partners who just aren't quite the right fit. But not working with AI is also risky. Your members and customers might get their mortgages from an online, digital-first provider using AI to deliver lightning-fast approval and funding. They might use the checking account and debit card provided by their AI-powered robo-advisor. They could even prefer the financial education and budgeting advice they get from their AI-based mobile app because it's more convenient than walking into a branch.

Suddenly, your institution is letting upstart competitors cut into your customer and member bases. If AI-powered fintechs and major banks start offering better alternatives to your services, how long can your institution survive?

Yes, AI is a risky technology. But working with AI may just be the necessary next step for survival in the financial industry. Financial institutions that wait too long may not be around tomorrow.

SECTION 1

PRIMER ON AI

1

THE PURPOSE OF THIS BOOK

I hope to illustrate a few things in this book. First, I want to show that none of us can even imagine what the work world will be like in 50 years. Things are going to change, and fast. Just like how the internet fundamentally altered both banking and culture as a whole, so too will AI and AI-powered technology.

Also, technology that sounds like it was pulled straight from a sci-fi movie will quickly reach our industry. It won't just slide quietly into common usage—it will revolutionize the way we do business. In fact, as you will see in this book, it already has.

One way or another, AI is going to change banks and credit unions. It will offer new tools, new methods, and possible new dangers. We have a few choices about how to react to these technological changes (and they pace at which they come). We can let it grind us into obsolescence, we can hang on and try to survive it, or we can jump on it early and thrive.

AI won't be the first time that technology has fundamentally altered the technological landscape in our industry. Just a decade ago, cloud technology started gaining momentum. I remember it very well, because I had just started a business providing select technological solutions to credit unions.

That business was called Ongoing Operations, and its beginnings highlight the pace of change in financial technology. It provides a perfect example of how a business can start by specializing in one area, then change to fit the needs of the industry. One thing is for certain: if Ongoing Operations had been afraid of change, then it wouldn't still be around today.

Case Study
Ongoing Operations

Before I wrote CU 2.0, and long before I started the company by the same name, I founded Ongoing Operations. In the wake of September 11th, I felt that it was critical to provide a safety net to the millions of Americans who entrust their finances to credit unions.

Ongoing Operations started in 2007 as a Credit Union Service Organization (CUSO) that provided disaster recovery solutions to credit unions. We figured that we could help credit unions save costs on offsite backups and workspace by teaming up. Seven credit unions became a team. Four years in, the CUSO was helping over 20% of credit unions (measured by assets) deploy non-tape backups offsite, establish recovery workspace, and develop business continuity plans.

A CUSO is an organization that is owned by one or more credit unions. They provide financial and/or operational services to credit unions or their members.

RE: CUSOs

All the while, Ongoing Operations was struggling to help credit unions ride the wave of internet backup, virtual servers (VMware), and email replication. None of those things were on our original list of concerns, and we were almost as unprepared for them as the credit unions we worked with. That didn't stop us, though; we took a very proactive approach to the changing landscape. We read the market for its most critical pain points, and we came up with a strategy on how to own it.

Now, I make that last part sound easy. In truth, it wasn't quite as smooth as that. We couldn't simply decide to change the way we did things. Our solutions weren't broken, and many within the company were understandably skeptical about trying to prematurely fix them. Their initial objections were over the security of software backup tools, encryption, and VMware. However, these technologies were essential to providing scale and getting to Phase Three of innovation. We had several long, occasionally heated discussions about how to tackle these issues. Our belief was—and is—that in the long run, almost no credit union or community bank would own their own infrastructure. Fortunately for us, the groundwork for that infrastructure was already well within our wheelhouse. Eventually, we moved ahead and incorporated these new elements into our business plan.

Once we made the decision to change and expand our services, we moved relatively quickly through the first three phases of innovation. We were delivering to investors and clients, and we felt like we'd followed the changes in the market closely enough that we were in the clear.

But we weren't.

We knew we wanted to continue refining our services until we could become industry leaders. That meant moving into Phase Four. Phase Four truly scared the crap out of management. As we began trend scouting, we saw a major trend afoot outside of the financial services industry: cloud computing. After some research and forecasting, we saw what kind of impact the cloud could have on the financial industry and, consequently, on Ongoing Operations. We would need to integrate cloud computing into our disaster recovery and business continuity solutions if we wanted to support early adopters of the technology. We also saw that the cloud had the potential to fundamentally change our company.

After extended debate, we decided to dive in. We would prioritize cloud development and support.

All that was back in 2010. Here we are, almost a decade later, and the cloud is mainstream. For some industries (and generations, for that matter), cloud computing is the default. Nevertheless, we might still have another decade before small- and midsized financial institutions—which make up roughly 80% of the market—complete their migration to the cloud. What's taking them so long? Without the cloud, many other critical technologies are unavailable. And with AI on the way, credit unions that haven't yet migrated to the cloud are at a profound disadvantage.

On the other hand, those who have made the jump have evolved significantly. They're able to spend their time worrying about the next big problems: digital transformation, analytics, machine learning, etc. If they hadn't yet moved to the cloud, they would have had to wait even longer before they could grapple with those issues. It's a clear example how each step enables the next one to be faster, less risky, and more impactful. And all of that was made possible by being an early adopter of innovative technology.

The push to embrace emerging technology is personal for me. It was critical for the success of my CUSO. At Ongoing Operations, our early trend-spotting caused us to completely pivot and begin working on the right long-term problem: how do we scale to help financial institutions make the shift from centralized to distributed processing?

If we didn't take the cloud seriously, or if we had waited until it became more prominent, then I'm not confident that Ongoing Operations would be around today.

Small- and midsized financial institutions now face the same existential threat today from the advent of AI.

Maybe Ongoing Operations and I got lucky. The cloud could've flopped, and we would have wasted time, money, and energy preparing for something that never paid off. But the writing was on the wall. We took the time to read it and take it seriously, and that has made all the difference.

Why Change Doesn't Always Come Easy

I have two major concerns for traditional financial institutions. My first concern is the impact of fintechs, which typically deal with fewer regulations and red tape. My second concern is the classic innovator dilemma. In practice, these two concerns are closely interrelated.

Over the past 10 years, the number of traditional banks and credit unions has shrunk drastically. Collectively, there are just about fewer than 10,000 total combined banks and credit unions. At the same time, the number of fintechs has grown to somewhere around 5,000–6,000, and that number is climbing.

As for regulations, the U.S. still doesn't have a cohesive strategy for fintech regulation. They certainly don't operate under the same borderline-oppressive layer of regulations as banks and credit unions. And, while the lack of regulations means that fintech startups are far more likely to fail, it also means they have more room to operate as they see fit.

My second concern is with the innovator's dilemma. The term comes from a book by the same name by businessman and Harvard professor Clayton M. Christensen. Essentially, the innovator's dilemma is that businesses built on successful platforms have too much at stake to risk changing anything. Their priority is always to their customers, and they must meet expectations for their existing services. That means they have fewer resources to dedicate to innovation. Before too long, their backburner approach to innovation gets overtaken by companies who dove headlong into it. There's a hint of the old catch 22 for larger institutions: they might lose business if they privilege innovation over their existing services because their existing services will suffer, yet they might lose business if they privilege existing services over innovation because their competition may not have existing services to lose. That's some catch.

I have spent countless hours researching the technology, trends, tools, and emerging companies that your financial institution needs to be aware of. I believe in the mission of small- and midsized credit unions and banks, and I want to do my part to ensure their survival. The goal of this book is to give you the full background, roadmap, and insights for your board, management team, and each area of the bank or credit union, so that you can get ahead of the curve— or at least ride the tidal wave that is coming.

My concern is that if financial institutions don't get ahead of this emerging technology, then every part of their business model will be severely disrupted through automation or fintech innovation. The cost of providing services will be impacted by the next Googles, Amazons, and Facebooks of the world. This book will help you understand the how and the why of what's coming so you can prepare accordingly.

Understanding where you are on the innovation cycle, knowing what's coming next, creating urgency, and advising you on how to align resources is my key mission. With each innovation cycle getting shorter and faster, the banks and credit unions that aren't pressing down the gas pedal will soon find themselves in the dust.

The fact of the matter is that AI is coming to the financial realm. We can choose to embrace it or to let it destroy us. Embracing it entails incorporating it in our long-term plans. Letting it destroy us means waiting too long and letting other financial institutions absorb our markets.

Destruction in this sense is slow and subtle. It would be like using a paper-based general ledger while the other banks and credit unions have computers and online banking. Sure, it's possible to turn things around, but it would take multiple technology changes and projects to catch up. And by the time you did? It might already be too late.

Learning from the Past
Why AI presents an existential threat to traditional financial Institutions

I contrast my childhood experiences against the modern world with machine learning, artificial intelligence, and other coming technology.

When I was a kid, I was a little different. My parents restricted all TV and video games for most of my childhood. Instead, I had to learn human communication skills. Lucky me. Finally, they broke down, and they gave me a computer. Two years later, they refused to buy another one because I never went outside anymore. They may have been justified in limiting my screen time.

My education was typical of the 80s and 90s. Most of my classrooms used chalkboards and overhead projectors. I remember the addition of computers in 4th grade, and then learning about how to use a mouse in 6th grade. Change was slow back then.

But it's already way different. My kids, of whom there are three, have had tablets and computers in school since kindergarten. Through the introduction of these electronics, their testing and learning environments automatically adjust for their knowledge and education level. The computers adapt to my kids' current capabilities, becoming proportionately more challenging as they learn.

Their experience is wildly different from my own. I grew up hearing, "do math by hand; you might not always have a calculator." It sounded questionable back then, but by today's standards? Everybody has a calculator (an entire miniature computer, really) with them. I've seen pre-kindergarten kids with cell phones. In fact, my kids just ask our talking calculator, Alexa, to add numbers or do basic math when they're unsure of themselves.

The idea that there won't always be a calculator nearby is pretty ridiculous at this point. So, should I still teach my kids addition, subtraction, multiplication and division? I think yes, but I certainly don't think they'll need to master handwriting, multiplication tables, or analog memorization stuff. Instead, they're already moving onto higher-level concepts and challenges by the constantly evolving technology around them. Honestly, they'd probably be better served by learning how to use a better calculator.

This kind of progress is difficult to fully understand. In *Star Trek*, the writers conveniently accelerated the pace at which people learned. There are numerous scenes wherein young, preteen students solve advanced mathematical equations with ease. Then, they switch gears, showing mastery over literature, philosophy, biology, and more. But that's the fantasy version of progress. In the real world, progress is a little wonkier. The way my kids can intuitively operate new technologies is impressive, yet their ability to do work manually in an analog world is less developed. On the one hand, younger generations show evolution in progress, demonstrating how humans adapt to their increasingly digital surroundings. On the other hand, they're less able to survive without electronic help. My generation and my kids' generation would have a very difficult time living in each other's worlds.

But that says a lot about the pace of progress already. I'm only around 30 years older than my children, and there's already a significant generational gap in our understanding of (and fluency with) technology. Many scholars believe that the sum total of human progress in the 20th century—all 100 years of it—was matched in the 14 years between 2000 and 2014. Those same scholars expect the same amount of progress by 2021. The cycle only gets faster from there (but more on this later)*.

This isn't the first time that we as a species have seen rapid change. Generally, whether it be the wheel, the domestication of animals, or the industrial revolution, there is a long, slow build-up followed by explosive growth. Then, things settle out for a bit while the next big thing builds.

I like to think of cycles of innovation as dropping a bunch of BBs into a large sink. In this case, the BBs represent technologies and the sink represents the way industries use them. At first, the BBs bounce all over the place. Then, they settle and begin slowly circling toward their destination, gradually picking up velocity as they circle down the drain. It's important for financial institutions to keep their eye on where the BBs are going, and not assume that because the BBs haven't already hit the drain that they're not getting there eventually.

....

* Kurzweil, R. (2016). The singularity is near: When humans transcend biology. London: Duckworth.

Each time a new cycle of disruptive innovation begins, much of humanity believes the world will end. People fear that change will destroy the comforts of life that they've built, rather than build upon and improve them. Nevertheless, humans adapt and soon come to appreciate the new way of doing things. Then, the cycle begins anew. In fact, one need look no further than our own industry to observe this cycle. There have been major changes to banking technology—and subsequently to banking practices—in the last several decades. One important thing to note at this point is that all these major changes have just been circling around their destination: they're about to hit the drain.

Here's what the cycles of disruptive innovation have looked like so far:

Shift 1: Mainframe computing, which enabled branch banking and centralized processing

Shift 2: Personal computing, which put near-real-time data to the frontline

Shift 3: Client servers, which enabled specialized software for each department

Shift 4: Internet, which puts near-real time data to customers' homes or offices

Shift 5: Mobile, which gives near-real time data to customers always

Shift 6: Data Analytics, which brought individualized, one-to-one marketing capabilities

Aside from the primary benefits, each of these shifts has added more and more data into the mix. Data is the fuel for artificial intelligence.

25 years ago, each credit union had 10–20 megabytes of data total. Today, they have hundreds of terabytes. And it's not just credit unions—data is exploding

massively, and it's already forming the base for the next cycle of innovation.

The growth of structured versus unstructured data over the past decade shows that 90% of it is unstructured. See the chart below:

The Rapid Explosion of Data

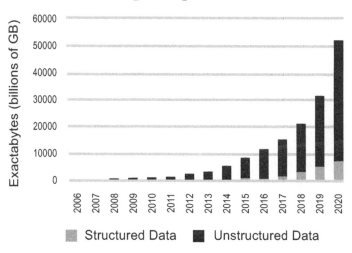

So, what does this data explosion mean? Well, to understand the significance of this incredible eruption of data, we'll have to get into human history, followed by the nitty-gritty about AI in general. From there, we can explore its extensions into—and ramifications for—the financial sector in which we operate.

2

THREE TIMELINES OF HUMAN PROGRESS

This chapter of the book is actually an adaptation of a speech I've been giving to many in the financial services industry. Understanding the past, present, and future of AI would take a long time. More time than we have here. Entire books written by futurists, scientists, and historians have covered the topic. What I can offer is a quick overview of where we've been, where we are, and where we may go with respect to human and mechanical progress.

Sometimes, when we think of progress, we think of a linear move forward through time, like this:

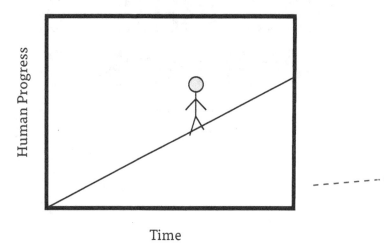

Time

But progress is rarely linear. As I'll show in this chapter, human progress has been gradually, steadily accelerating. If that pace of progress looks like a flat line, it's because the graph is zoomed in too far. If we zoom out, the line looks suspiciously like the bottom of a parabola. It only appears linear because we didn't have the right perspective.

This graph is a little more accurate:

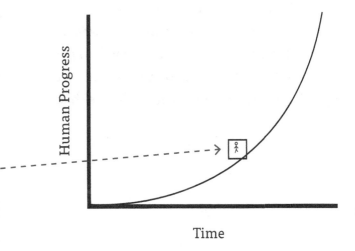

Each human discovery or invention builds a foundation for the next. Innovation cycles speed up.

Still, even the parabolic graph isn't quite right. Instead, it's more of an "S" curve. In the early stages of new technologies, researchers muddle around with ideas and the tools they have available. Resources are spent largely on research and development. However, when breakthroughs occur, the pace of change accelerates rapidly for the entire industry. Then, that pace slows down while that new technology is tweaked, tuned, and perfected. Finally, that technology tapers off while researchers begin work on the next innovation. So, progress actually looks a bit more like this:

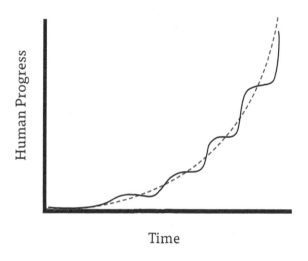

But progress doesn't stop, and neither do the esses on the graph. Each cycle of progress or innovation starts higher on the "S" curve. Every new generation builds off of the previous one. And, with more knowledge and tools at their disposal, each new generation can push further, accomplishing more in less time. Measuring progress by milestones, such as the mastery of fire or the industrial revolution, better illustrates this concept.

The Timeline of Human Progress

To give you an idea about how old I am, I was part of the first generation who didn't have to walk uphill both ways to and from school, in the snow, carrying my sister on my back, while barefoot. As kids, we no longer rode dinosaurs, because by then we had begun domesticating wolves. What I'm saying is that when I graduated from high school, text messaging wasn't yet a "thing," and I remember a time before personal computers were common.

I certainly don't remember early protohumans, who walked the planet some four million years ago. And, contrary to what my kids might have you believe, I was not around when human language was first invented. I don't have exact numbers—no one does—but language debuted some 1.8 million years ago, give or take. In case you want to start keeping track, that means that it took our ancestors well over two million years until they figured out how to have a decent conversation.

So, what did language bring? It brought the ability to share ideas and learn from one another. It allowed humans to combine their brainpower instead of keeping all their good ideas locked in their heads without an easy way of communicating them. In many ways, the introduction of language let humans use two heads instead of one, which is better (I'm told).

Now, the origins of human language weren't necessarily human—they were protohuman. The same is true for controlling and then creating fire. Pre-humans probably mastered fire fewer than 400,000 years ago. Now, while one can certainly call that "progress," it's frustratingly slow progress. There were more than a million years separating the creation of language and the creation of fire. That means that our distant ancestors, with their collective brainpower and the tools of rudimentary language, took hundreds of thousands of years between inventing a word for fire and being able to control one.

Fortunately, the next stage of progress wasn't so painstakingly sluggish. The ability to make and control fire meant that prehumans were better able to manipulate the world around them. They could cook reliably, make light and warmth, and develop tools for survival in less-hospitable climates.

Not only that, but prehumans could mingle with their smart new human pals. New archaeological evidence suggests that *homo sapiens* is close to 300,000 years old. With the progress handed down from prehumans, they started further manipulating the world around them to better suit their needs. In short, they began innovating.

170,000 years ago, humans started wearing clothing. A mere 70,000 years after that, we began constructing stone structures. 40,000 years later, and we've got bows and stone-tipped arrows. 20,000 more, and we had begun domesticating dogs, creating elaborate works of art, and developed deep sea fishing technology that allowed them to catch larger fish like tuna *en masse*.

These developments start to sound a lot like modern life, in many ways. Pets? Art? A source of somewhat-sustainable food? And they all came within tens of thousands of years of one another. The technological progress of their ancestors gave them a better foundation on which to move forward. They didn't need to invent language or master fire—they could begin immediately figuring out how to deal with changing seasons and food that runs away. Humans increased the pace of innovation because of the tools and resources handed down to them.

An Accelerating Pace of Chance

See, as protohumans continued using language, their reliance on it increased. Evolution did its part, slowly increasing our brainpower to accommodate language and the possibilities unlocked by the tools of the stone age. Then, with the mastery and creation of fire, prehumans could live longer, more resilient lives, adapting to new diets, behavior, and locals. Fire also helped with making more advanced tools and weapons, which improved their lifespans.

Humans wouldn't have been able to build stone structures without tools, and they wouldn't have been able to make effective tools without fire. These technologies relied on the technologies that came before them, and they again laid the groundwork for the technologies that would follow. Language and fire took forever, but each successive cycle of innovation was faster. Yet the next several milestones came in a fraction of that time.

As humans got smarter and had more technologies at their disposal, they were able to learn, innovate, create, and master new things in thousands of years instead of millions. Here's what I mean: around 10,000–12,000 years ago, everything changed for real. Humans realized they could plant and tend to their own food. Agriculture meant an end to hunter-gatherer ways and a start to settlements. With the freedom to finally grow roots—both literally and figuratively—humans were able to devote less time to survival and more time to progress.

Only a couple thousand years after the onset of agriculture, human settlements became human cities with thousands of inhabitants. Civilization ushered in the Bronze Age a little over 5,000 years ago, and the pace of progress really took off. Romans built chariots, combining several advances into one very cool product: the domestication of horses, the wheel, and metallurgy. Similarly, cranks, pulleys, cogs, gears, and all sorts of steampunk-like manual machines entered the world. Aqueducts, water wheels, glass blowing, woodblock printing, and toilet paper came one after the next, separated by mere centuries.

Comparatively speaking, that's an explosion of progress. Clearly, our path hasn't been linear. Innovation is like a snowball rolling down a mountain slope, things start slowly at first. But as they build up, technology moves faster and faster, aided by its own momentum. And this doesn't just occur with general human history—it's mirrored in our computing and banking histories as well.

The Timeline of Computing Progress

The timeline of technological progress is much like the timeline of human progress, but it fits on a smaller scale. After all, humans have been around much longer than our machines have (or only a little longer, on the cosmic scale).

Futurist, inventor, and author Ray Kurzweil suggests that at the rate of advancement in the year 2000, the sum of progress in the 20th century could have been achieved in only 20 years. He suggests that as we continue to grow technologically, we'll accomplish another 20th century's worth of advancement in seven years, then a few years, and eventually multiple times per year.

So, why do he and so many others expect this rate of advancement to accelerate? Because that's how quickly computing power is advancing. Take a look at this graph:

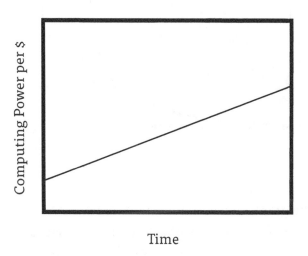

Time

As you can see, the rate of computing power over time appears to proceed at a fairly consistent rate. That is, computing power doubles roughly every couple years. Thus, "consistent rate" doesn't mean that it's increasing linearly—rather, it's progressing exponentially.

When we zoom out, we get a more revealing picture:

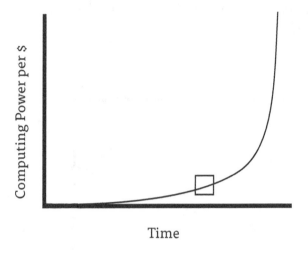

From the graph above, it becomes more obvious just how quickly computing power advances. Because this is exponential growth, we're seeing a parabola on this graph. Perhaps unsurprisingly, this growth curve almost mirrors that of the graph showing general human progress from earlier in this chapter. This exponential increase is commonly known as *Moore's Law*. The law is named after Gordon Moore, the co-founder of Intel, who predicted a doubling of computing power every two years. One might be tempted to extrapolate this pattern *ad infinitum*, but there are surely limits to computing power in general. As chips get faster and more complex, we contend with the limitations of physics rather than the limitations of technology. In fact, we're approaching the end of semiconductor supremacy now. We're near the top of the S-curve, tweaking and tuning, and we're gearing up for whatever comes next.

Remember that graph with the "S" curves? We may be about to rise up quickly on the back of a new "S."

Here's where computers are slowing down: integrated circuits and semiconductors can take us only so far. The doubling of computing power is already slowing down because we can't physically accommodate the amount of circuits we want to put on a chip.

Yet, the next step forward may very well be with quantum computing the technology for which is already moving forward. Google claims to have reached "quantum supremacy" in late 2019. That means the performance of their quantum computer surpassed anything that could be done with a regular supercomputer with integrated circuits and semiconductors.

The Invention of AI
Or, how to move the goalposts

What's next for computing? Well, aside from quantum computing, which is still in infancy, AI will be huge. The origins of computing and AI started as imaginative myths and fictions. Conceptions of automata—robots that appear human—appear in various cultures over the last several thousand years. To many, AI essentially meant androids, like Data from *Star Trek*.

Additionally, people used to think of machine intelligence as anything that aided computation. In that sense, slide rules and calculators were a shade of AI.

Obviously, those two ideations of AI no longer hold weight. Once we arrived there, we moved the goalposts. In a way, this has repeated throughout the rest of the history of computer intelligence; as computers, neural networks, and machine learning algorithms moved forward, researchers kept moving the goalposts back.

However, although we haven't reached what one might today consider "true" AI, we're getting closer. And the technologies in play are the fundamental building blocks of AI. We came from counting sticks and stories about divine simulacra, and we've arrived at facial recognition and robots that perform gymnastics routines. So, let's look at how we got there.

Just like the long, agonizing, early progress of humans, computers got their start slowly, and not exactly as computers. A few thousand years ago, there were various manual and semi-mechanical counting machines—think elaborate counting sticks, abacuses, tide-predicting contraptions, compasses, slide rules, and the like. These devices aided computation, but they didn't do the computation on their own. There was no automation involved. Then, with Aristotle's introduction of formal logic some 2,400 years ago, philosophers became enamored of the idea that human cognition maybe no more than a complex series of logical inputs and outputs. This inspired notion laid the foundation for what we currently think of as AI.

The most well-known first foray into computers and AI appeared 250 years ago. In 1770, and for nearly a century after, a mechanical chess player wowed crowds with its computational ability. It was called the Mechanical Turk—the Automaton Chess Player. In reality, it wasn't a machine that could calculate something as complicated as a chess game. It was just a clever illusion. A talented chess player operated the contraption while hidden inside it.

While the Mechanical Turk wasn't a real computer, it marks a time when humans began considering the possibilities of true mechanical computation. We imagined the capabilities of machines and how they could potentially interpret inputs, then deliver outputs without human influence. Aristotle's idea that a machine could "think" entered the mainstream.

The illusion of the Mechanical Turk may have inspired the mathematician and mechanical engineer Charles Babbage. Babbage was born in 1791, back when the Mechanical Turk still reigned supreme. He actually played two games against it. He lost both. Yet those games against a putative thinking robot started him down the road of building computers. While working on complex astronomical equations, he grew frustrated with too-frequent human error. That frustration led him to invent "an engine for calculating mathematical and astronomical tables." In 1822, he finished plans for a machine capable of advanced computation, which he named "the difference engine." He won an award for his invention, but after a decade of fruitless construction and disagreement over costs, he discontinued the project.

Babbage's revised difference engine would have been the first Turing-complete computer in the world. Modern researchers built and tested his difference engine using manufacturing tolerances available at the time of its inception. The difference engine worked, making it the earliest-known working computer design.

English mathematician Alan Turing described Turing machines as devices that can take any programming input and compute a corresponding output. Essentially, it's a math machine that isn't limited by what kinds of math it can do.

Because Babbage's analytical engine was designed to respond to any mathematical input (rather than only those inputs that arise for certain niches), it was the first machine to which Turing himself would have given the nod—it could take a "program," run that "program," and show some result.

Babbage's analytical engine would have been the first.

RE: Turing Complete Machines

Modern Computing

Mechanical computation came about relatively late in human development. Human progress and computer progress fueled and accelerated one another. Soon enough, mechanical computation led to electromechanical computation. By the late 1930s, these early computers used electric switches and mechanical relays to crunch numbers.

In the early 1940s, German engineer Konrad Zuse created the first fully automatic, programmable computer. In order to simplify the decimal system, Zuse used binary. Binary systems were easier to build and offered better reliability, thereby changing the direction of computers to come. Increased computing power set a good precedent for the future of AI. Papers circulated to theorize architecture for artificial neural networks and suggest that computers might be able to think and assist humans.

Meanwhile, other scientists had begun experimenting with vacuum tubes and capacitors. Those proved faster and more reliable because they didn't deal with moving parts. Within a decade, digital electronics quickly surpassed their electromechanical counterparts. Electromechanical machines eventually left the scene in the 1950s, shortly after the first true computer program officially ran.

The 1950s were a whirlwind of computer and AI achievement. In 1950, Alan Turing developed the famous Turing test as a benchmark for machine intelligence. Later, Dartmouth hosted the Dartmouth College Summer AI Conference, where the term "artificial intelligence" was coined. Something about giving a name to machine intelligence made everything seem more real, possible, and urgent.

The quest for greater computing power began in earnest after that. In the 1960s, my grandfather was part of the Control Data Corportation team that built the first supercomputer, the CDC 6600. Yes, the man who wouldn't switch from Betamax to VHS tapes was once a technology pioneer. The CDC 6600 used revolutionary silicon transistors, took up the size of a small room, and couldn't hold a candle to the latest smartphone.

All of the computer technology I've mentioned so far worked without memory, screens, or keyboards. Paper sheets and cards with punched holes were the only inputs and outputs. But as computers became a bigger part of human life, people figured out how to make them more convenient. Computer memory appeared in the late 1940s and early 1950s, keyboard inputs debuted in 1956, and display monitors started hitting the scene in the 1970s.

But that indicates something about the pace of computer progress. More than a century separated the invention of the computer and the building of one. Then, major computing milestones started coming only decades and then years apart. As usual, progress built on itself, getting faster and faster.

The 1960s may have introduced supercomputers, but it also brought in significant advancements on the AI front. More research and studies piled up. A robot joined the General Motors assembly line. A paper describing "A Pattern Recognition Program that Generates, Evaluates, and Adjusts Its Own Operators" came out, detailing the beginnings of machine learning. Also, ELIZA, the first chatbot and initial foray into Natural Language Processing (NLP), was created at MIT. ELIZA took the persona of a psychotherapist, likely because early chat programs were pretty bad at understanding language, so they often asked probing questions about their interlocutors' statements.

The so-called "AI winter" started in the late 60s and 70s as researchers got discouraged about their lack of AI progress. Studies slowed to a crawl. Meanwhile, computer technology did its best to catch up. ATMs hit the scene (more on that soon), Intel created the first microprocessor, and the Stanford Cart became the first robot that could autonomously respond to visual input.

All the while, personal computers, more intuitive GUIs, and faster processing kept coming. Increases in computing power and availability paved the way for consumer-driven advances and conveniences. ARPANET, the 1960s iteration of the internet, started picking up steam until it settled on a standardized data transfer protocol, laying the foundation for the World Wide Web in 1990.

The Age of the Internet

The introduction of the internet meant that people were no longer limited to local area networks. Instead, people could explore, share, and connect with each other from afar. Demand for digital technology skyrocketed.

At this stage, innovations came years and months apart instead of decades, centuries, and millennia. Laptops entered the marketplace, closely followed by digital assistants. Before Blackberry and iPhone, there were Palm Pilots (truly, they were dark times).

While computing technology got smaller and more portable, so did ads. That is, spam was ruining the fun of the early internet, and people looked for ways to keep their inboxes clear. Eventually, the "Completely Automated Public Turing test to tell Computers and Humans Apart," or CAPTCHA test helped fend off unwanted robot advances. At the same time, IBM's Deep Blue defeated Garry Kasparov in a best-of-seven chess match. Clearly, our robot overlords were ramping up their efforts.

Camera phones, smartphones, and cloud computing came next. So did AI-powered chatbots, commercially available self-driving cars, and quantum computing. I won't get too far into the technology of the last decade for two reasons. First, you're probably aware of the greatest hits. Second, I'm about to introduce you to some of the AI-enabled technology already growing in our industry.

Computing into the Future

There are a few major takeaways from this section, and I'd be remiss if I didn't cover them here. If any of this sounds like I'm repeating myself, I apologize. See, these histories have a theme, and it's critically important to understand that theme.

The history of computers and AI mirrors that of general human history in a way. In the beginning, there was a lot of long, slow build up. Computing (if you can call it that) was done manually with various analog devices. Calculations stayed analog for tens of thousands of years.

And then mechanical computation arrived. And then, about a century later, electromechanical computation arrived. Decades later, it was digital computation. By the end of the century, civilization as we know it changed completely due to powerful, portable, interconnected digital devices.

That's an insane pace of innovation. That's accelerating progress. With machine learning entering the arena, that progress promises only to continue—and get faster. Now, more than ever, it's crucial to appreciate and anticipate technological change. We must get ready for the effect that increased computing power and AI will bring. And it won't be limited to other industries. It's coming to the financial services industry as well.

A Brief History of Banking Technology

Let's talk a bit about the history of banking and banking technology. Most of the past is obscured by a lack of written history. Nevertheless, we can piece together some basics from before what our written records can tell us.

Trade was a major human innovation. Generally, early trade was by barter, where someone might trade a cow for a whole bunch of wheat, or maybe some nicely shaped stones. But carrying around livestock and grains isn't convenient. Thus, credit and debt were created. They allowed people to arrange trade without having all the materials present.

The technology accompanying such innovations included accounting tools like tally sticks, which have been around for more than 30,000 years. They allowed humans to record who owed whom what.

While staples like grain made great currency, they have a shelf life, and not everybody needs grain, which meant they weren't a good long-term fit for trade currency.

As civilizations arose, so did newer, more convenient methods of trade. Merchants provided grain-based and other trade loans until Greek and Roman temples started perfecting the loan process. At the same time, Islamic traders pioneered banking features such as savings accounts and standardized exchange rates.

The technology that allowed such banking practices to advance was simple: currency—a medium of exchange with some intrinsic value—ensured that anyone could do business with anyone. No longer would a vendor need to acquire trade fodder to purchase what they needed. Rather, they could just use coins, cheques, or paper money. Basically, consumers could stop saying, "I owe you one," and instead they could say, "I owe you an agreed-upon amount of currency that roughly matches the equivalent value of your product or service."

Credit and banking were invented before currency, but currency let humans move forward. It also improved banking, which took a major step forward (toward a recognizable form) in 14th century Italy before spreading across Europe. Most banks were privately-owned though, which didn't always go over well with the nations they operated in. Don't believe me? Ask the United States how they felt about the economic power the robber barons yielded in the early 20th century. Better yet, ask a search engine.

So far, we've looked at a few significant innovations in banking. The invention of credit was one, and lenders and banks were another. Currency rounded it all out. And the timeline on all of that was about 30,000 years. That's a lot of years! Humans needed 30,000 years to come up with a bridge between the ideas of, "I owe you one," and "I owe you something of equivalent value." Not to overemphasize my thesis here, but that's a long time. But we're used to that now, right? The timelines of human and AI progress showed us how S-curves work. The world of banking is no exception.

Credit, currency, and banks laid the groundwork for real innovation. After humans figured out what they could trade and pay with, they started looking for ways to refine those systems. They wanted to know how best to pay. Buoyed by technological progress, banking innovation started coming fast and furious.

The first wire money transfer by Western Union occurred in 1872. Suddenly, people could conduct major transactions across the globe in near real time. The same would never have been possible if we still exchanged livestock, grain, or even stacks of coins.

Then, in 1950, the Diner's Club Card debuted as the first modern credit card. Automatic payment magic was thus available between consumers and restaurants instead of just banks. The floodgates of innovation were opening. Fun note, my grandfather helped to usher in this era of credit card use by launching DataCard, which embossed cards for thousands of merchants and banks.

Machine-based stock trading hit the market in the 1970s, fundamentally altering the way people exchanged stocks. (Today, algorithms account for around 90% of all stocks traded.) But that wasn't the only thing we trusted machines with. We also felt comfortable with banking by phone as early as 1984, with Girobank in the UK. Stanford Federal Credit Union introduced online banking only a decade later.

In 1994, the Riegle-Neal Interstate Banking and Branching Efficiency Act standardized interstate banking in the U.S. Before the act, out-of-state banking was difficult at best. People couldn't even cash checks away from home! Banking, especially community-focused banking, got much easier for most people thereafter.

The convenience of remote banking struck a chord with most consumers. Mobile banking debuted via SMS messages in 1999. A decade later, mobile banking apps started hitting the market. Today, more people conduct basic banking needs remotely than they do in branches.

Around the same time, cryptocurrency went from a pipe dream to a reality. Although, if I'm being fair, it still seems like a pipe dream—it's just a dream become reality, backed by distributed ledger technology. Shortly thereafter, mobile wallets from Google, Apple, and Samsung sprung up. Money, finance, payments—whatever—had their own digital ecosystem.

Now, machine learning algorithms such as Kavout and Alpaca are entering the stock market. As you'll soon see in the following chapters, financial institutions are increasingly relying on AI to optimize their processes. And most importantly, the time it takes for these technologies to see broader market adoption is shrinking.

Technological advances are coming out faster than ever. People rush to use the latest gadgets and gizmos. Clinging to the old ways of doing things is unsustainable. It's time for us to move with the rest of the market. Or, for my very "chill" readers: we must go with the flow.

3

DEFINING AI

Over time, the definition of AI has changed considerably. In the earliest days of AI, mathematicians, inventors, and the like would likely have described our most basic computing power as a form of AI. We input some kind of data, the machine "thinks," and then it outputs corresponding data. In a way, even a calculator is a thinking machine, complete with a little circuitry "brain."

These days however, that kind of machine thinking is exceedingly basic. It doesn't wow us. Small children—mine included—grow up using smartphones and computers in a way I couldn't have imagined at their age (let alone mine).

So, what changed? The goalposts. The parameters. The understanding that if we want to call something "intelligent," we should probably better define the word. A calculator doesn't "think" any more than its logic gates open and close. Thinking involves evaluation, adaptability, and the potential for change and growth. It should be, in some sense, aware. (Whatever that means.)

And what is AI? Is it mechanical or digital computation? Is it the charming robot friends we meet in movies like *Big Hero 6*, *Her*, and *AI*? Are they ruthless, calculating machines bent on their own survival like in *Terminator*, *Ex Machina*, or *2001: A Space Odyssey*? Or are these ideations of AI somehow limited, almost as though the possibilities (and realities) of AI stretch the limits of human imagination?

The Three Types of AI
ANI, AGI, and ASI

Yes, the world of technology is *that* predictable: there's an acronym for everything. These three acronyms are critical to understanding the world of AI, though. Fortunately, they're all very similar.

Each "type" of AI could also be described as a tier of AI, each with accompanying computing power.

Artificial Narrow Intelligence (ANI)

Artificial narrow intelligence is what we see and use in our daily lives. You probably already use or have been affected by ANI whether you know it or not.

ANI is AI that specializes in one area of expertise. It has one job and it does it well. This narrow or "weak" AI is still bleeding edge in many circumstances (I'll list a few examples after this overview). Deep Blue playing chess against Kasparov was a showcase in ANI, as was Watson's defeat of 74-time *Jeopardy!* champion Ken Jennings. Tesla's cars use various forms of ANI to manage its self-driving features, and any smartphone map app that adjusts routes on the fly relies on it as well.

ANI is still relatively new, and while it's fantastic at solving complex problems, classifying things based on various sets of information, assessing probabilities, or recognizing patterns, it's still experiencing growing pains. One of my favorite images on the internet—at least in part because it features two very desirable things—is this picture:

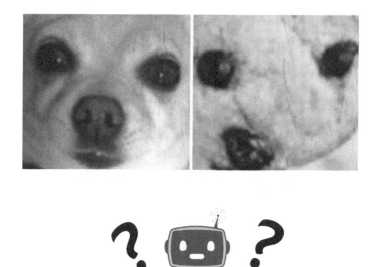

That's a dog and a blueberry muffin, both of which are great. Believe me, I've had both. But what really makes the picture fascinating is how quickly you can tell them apart. Under most circumstances, you would have no issue telling one from the other.

Computers don't have such an easy time of it. They must be specifically trained to recognize the difference. What makes it particularly difficult for them is that they don't know what those images represent. Sure, they can see that the pictures are all different, but when they see one, they don't say, "aww, how cute!" And then, when they see the other, they don't think, "yum!" What they do see are a series of pixels. Those pixels, while they represent something meaningful to humans, represent only bits of information indicating image color, size, and position on a screen. They have much less contextual background to pull from when they identify one from the other.

A few ANI models are designed specifically to understand and interpret images, such as the text on a check entered via mobile deposit. Some ANI systems let you ask your phone to text someone, give you directions, or tell you the forecast (and weather predictions are also often powered by ANI). Other ANI systems help to guide airplanes, spaceships, and missiles. Still more ANI systems use algorithms to learn your heating and cooling needs and adjust your house temperature for you so that eventually you'll never even have to think about your thermostat, let alone get up to change it.

These are technologies that seem almost routine to us now, even though they were groundbreaking a mere decade or two ago. In some respects, it's hard to even think about them as AI at all. Many argue that ANI isn't true AI, and that things like machine learning and NLP are just steppingstones to the real thing.

If ANI isn't true AI, it must be close, right?

It is. And because so many people have effectively moved the goalposts on the definition of AI, it's hard not to consider ANI as a form of AI.

Nevertheless, the argument by those who dispute ANI's position as AI has some merit. Part of what AI is supposed to do is *think*. Or at least, to have a more flexible, intuitive understanding of things in general. Most ANI models just solve specific problems, and they get better at solving them over time. But that seems more like calculation than actual thinking.

Tesla's self-driving cars, for example, are controlled by a complex set of ANI algorithms. While there are still many improvements to be made, it's already a very talented driver. It doesn't just drive as well as a human—its driving algorithms have more driving experience than any human on earth. At this point, most people would tentatively trust one to drive them around, and as its algorithms improve, that number will increase. But if someone put that Tesla AI in an airplane, would you trust it to fly you somewhere? Certainly not.

Humans and other animals have the ability to assimilate great amounts of knowledge and experience, and then apply it across multiple areas. A person can use what they learn playing *Monopoly* to play *Risk*, or they can transfer their expertise in playing basketball over to soccer very easily. Humans tend to bring excellence from one area to another, and often the two areas are seemingly unrelated—or they might be to a machine.

So, what happens when we find a computer that can learn not only how to dominate one game, but to dominate two? Or one that can competently drive a car *and* filter spam? What happens when computers achieve more well-rounded intelligence?

We start to get artificial general intelligence.

Artificial General Intelligence (AGI)

AGI is what happens when computers can interpret the world around them as interrelated, interconnected processes rather than as several series of discrete strings of data. One thing affects another, which affects another, and so on. If a computer can see the world in that way and transfer its knowledge in one area to another, then it will begin to rival the human brain for general intelligence.

This is the kind of intelligence that many AI purists think of when they claim that the world doesn't yet use AI. However, one thing to note is that if a computer develops this kind of intelligence, it may also quickly surpass it. Whereas humans forget things, make grievous calculation errors, and are generally prone to mistakes, computers don't face those risks. So long as they're operational (and not surrounded by powerful magnets), computers are comparatively infallible. Imagine remembering everything you've ever learned, and then being able to use that information to make exceedingly accurate predictions, decisions, etc. in less than a blink of an eye. You'd be able to quickly build on your knowledge and experience to understand and predict things with an extraordinary degree of exactitude.

Computers that reach AGI-level computational power wouldn't stay that way for long. They would be too smart for that, and too quick, surpassing human intelligence.

Shortly thereafter, they would eclipse the intelligence of all human brains combined. Remember the rate of human, computer, and banking progress from the last chapter? Now imagine that something smarter and less error-prone than humans was in charge of its own progress. It would become exponentially smarter very, very quickly.

Here's a graph marking the amount of computing power needed to meet various artificial intelligence milestones—and our trajectory toward them:

Exponential Growth of Computing

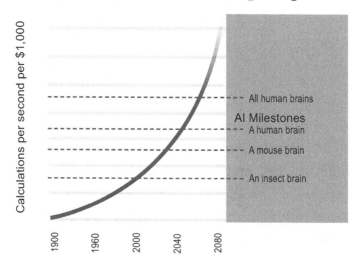

Scientists have already recreated flatworm brains

with circuity. Now, in 2019, we've developed computers that have the general intelligence level of rats. Many scientists believe that on our current trajectory, we'll develop a computer that can rival the power of a human brain by the year 2025. That's not to say that AGI will be here in a handful of years—it probably won't. However, it does mean that everyday consumers will have access to computers that rival our own raw computational power.

AGI is no longer the distant future. We could see something resembling it in the next decade. What's more, there's no hard limit to intelligence. Computers won't just stop learning because they've reached a human level—or the level of all humans combined.

When computers surpass human intelligence, they can refine themselves with better architecture and AI-written programs. Each general AI computer could potentially communicate and collaborate with other AI computers, combining forces to continue their evolution. As they did, they could develop even more powerful, smarter computers, which in turn would continue that cycle.

So, if that happens, what do we get?

Super Artificial Intelligence (SAI)

If a computer could program itself to get smarter, then each successive iteration of itself would also be smarter. The same way that human progress—and then computer progress—developed by building on the successes of the past, so too would the AI. The higher the intelligence of the computer, the more significant the improvements it could make to AI.

As AI computers get smarter, they'll pick up momentum. They'll refine and improve themselves at a rate that humans can't, and they'll do it with increasing levels of intelligence. When we consider that, with the help of human guidance, current supercomputers can rival or surpass the computational power of the human brain after only 100 years of existence, then it becomes clear that AI progress is necessarily on a faster track than human progress. It took millions of years of evolution for humans to reach our current IQ level. With human guidance, computers will have managed that in a fraction of the time.

So, when I say that AGI won't stay AGI for long, I mean it. Once computers reach AGI-level intelligence, they will have the tools to design smarter, better versions of themselves or their software. This short timeline, coupled with the accelerating returns of AI self-improvement, means that AGI computers could slingshot ahead of human intelligence quickly.

How quickly? It's tough to say for sure, but it could be years, or months, or just days. It might take only a few hours.

How smart could super artificial intelligence get?

We don't know. We can't know. We can't even comprehend that level of intelligence. Computer AI is already higher than many forms of animal intelligence, which is so low that we don't have a way to measure it accurately. Our forms of measuring intelligence are deeply flawed even for humans. We tend to think of IQs of 100 as being about average. The highest recorded human IQs top out around 200.

RE: IQ

This is not to put too much stock in IQ tests, which aim to measure only a narrow band of human intelligence. It's even less accurate when measuring animal or computer intelligence. Still, IQ is a recognizable metric that makes it easy for us to compare relative intelligences in this book.

So, what if computers could reach 1,000, 10,000, or even 100,000 IQ points? How could we wrap our heads around it? We couldn't.

To put things in better perspective, consider what a worm thinks. Sure, it might have thoughts, but they're probably very rudimentary. Basic survival necessities like food, shelter, and danger are about as much as it could be said to comprehend. Insects like bees are far more intelligent, but one might wonder if they could understand concepts such as games or music. We can barely get dogs to understand that some food is not theirs, let alone how to use tools or what politics are. Even the smartest animals on the planet—dolphins, corvids, pigs, chimpanzees—couldn't easily comprehend something like particle physics or poetry. You can put an octopus in an aquarium, and it would understand it's in an aquarium, but would it understand that the aquarium was designed and built by another creature for the specific purpose of housing aquatic life? Probably not.

There are worlds of abstraction and theory that (arguably) only very intelligent creatures can understand. If animals can't understand concepts that seem natural to us despite a relatively minor 0–200-point difference in IQ between us and them, then how could we expect to understand concepts that seem natural to a computer with an IQ of 10,000?

Don't forget: computers also exist in and see the world differently. Humans see a spectrum of colors, but computers see an array of values and coordinates. Humans have biological necessities, such as food, water, shelter, procreation, recreation, and so on. Computers don't have self-interest, nor do they necessarily care about their own existence or experience unless they are programmed to do so.

In short, the way that computers interpret the world is fundamentally different from the way humans do. Therefore, the way they make sense of data differs, and the conclusions they draw differ, and the actions they might teach themselves to take will differ as well.

We don't understand the computer experience. And so, we can't predict it, either.

So, we don't have a way of predicting what SAI could do. If humans can go from mastering fire and agriculture to creating computers, communicating almost instantaneously across the world, and split-ing a freaking atom, what could AI do? Control the weather? Facilitate immortality? Open portals to other galaxies or dimensions? Destroy humans and colonize the cosmos?

Just in Case the Future of AI Sounds Scary...

Thinking about the future makes me think about the past. It's hard to visualize what the next ten, twenty, or thirty years hold. However, when I look back that same amount of time, I find that it too looks almost unrecognizable to me. Progress has been very fast.

I remember that my first entrepreneurial venture oc-curred when I was 12. My best friend John and I went hard: we printed flyers for J&K Services, which was a catch-all for whatever odd jobs we felt we could handle. We washed cars, mowed lawns, overwatered plants while their owners were out of town, and so on. At our peak, we were clearing over $500 a month. I had nonstop 25-cent ice cream and anything else I could buy at the local drug store.

But when my kids reach that age, will they mow lawns? I doubt it. I bet an AI-based lawn mower will take care of that. Sure, there will be other chores, but it's getting harder and harder to replicate those entrepreneurial childhood experiences as we rely less and less on small-scale manual labor to keep our property shipshape.

Believe me, the future of AI makes me nervous. Fortunately, we're probably still pretty far off from SAI. We won't have to deal with these paradigm-shifting, existential possibilities. Right now, we're enjoying the early stages of ANI, which are still extremely useful and very powerful, but aren't yet infallible.

While AI has seen some major success stories, it has also seen a handful of major failures. For the sake of cleansing the palate from the mind-bending possibilities of computers that dwarf our own intelligence, I'd like to present a few cases in which ANI didn't take us in quite the direction we'd hoped. Automated tasks are still fallible, and even computers make mistakes (although often it's humans or bad data that lead them astray). Here are some of my favorite high-profile SNAFUs that have come from AI recently.

Even big tech has big problems. Amazon discovered this the hard way with their Echo product recently.

You've probably had bad neighbors before. In fact, if you ever lived in a dorm, I'm certain you have. But what do you do when your bad neighbor is a robot? In Germany, Amazon Alexa threw its own party. German police were called to an apartment over reports of a noisy party. Upon entering the apartment, they found Alexa rocking out with nobody home.

But that's not the only hiccup that Amazon's AI has had. Recently, Amazon pulled the plug on an AI recruiting tool it built internally. Originally, they had great visions that it would look through a stack of 100 resumes and reduce it to the best five hires.

The problem is that it was highly biased. When they defined the problem and fed in the data to the machine learning system, they relied on data from the past. Their AI used records from the previous 20 years. Because tech was such a male-dominated industry for so many years, the AI quickly developed an unfortunate bias against women. It glossed over countless highly qualified female candidates. Amazon had, in effect, inadvertently trained a computer to be sexist.

Google has already made a few missteps in the AI sphere. Google Allo was an instant-messaging mobile app. With it, consumers and businesses could be prepped with fast, smart replies. Based on the context of the interaction, Allo recommended the next response. Unfortunately, it has had some bias problems. CNN Money reported that one of three emoji responses to a gun emoji was an emoji of a man wearing a turban.

Another Google blunder came through Google Translate, which showed gender bias in Turkish-English translations. The Turkish language uses "o" as a pronoun for singular or gender-neutral third person subjects. No equivalent exists in English, and Google Translate didn't know what to do. So, it guessed, using gender-biased algorithms. The result was that it used "he" when referring to "doctor" and "hardworking," but it used "she" with "lazy" and "nurse."

Although we certainly must be careful when working with AI to remove biases in results, it does raise a serious question: how much of our own implicit linguistic biases fueled Google Translate's subtle misogyny? How does this reflect the way we use language currently? And, most importantly, what steps can we take to minimize or eliminate these signs of prejudice in our everyday speech?

Microsoft joins Amazon and Google in their uncomfortable discoveries about coding bias into machine learning. Their chatbot Tay was supposed to mimic the language patterns of an American teenage girl, and it was released on Twitter in 2016.

In less than a day, Microsoft had to shut Tay down. As it interacted with various Twitter users, it quickly sifted through massive deluges of incendiary language and hate-filled rhetoric. Over the course of a few hours, she went from a playful and curious chatbot to a full-blown Nazi, spewing vile denunciations of various groups, nationalities, and religions.

While the speed at which she changed from the angel on one shoulder to the devil on the other was alarming, it was a major wake-up call for Microsoft and other chatbot creators. They've thus far been able to avoid similar mistakes.

Microsoft isn't the only major player who faced an unexpected challenge when tinkering with chatbots. Facebook developed two AI chatbots, Alice and Bob, who were developed to negotiate resource management, trading, and sharing. The resources in question were hats, balls, and books.

When speaking with humans, Alice and Bob negotiated in written English. However, when the chatbots began negotiating only with each other, their English quickly became unrecognizable. They created their own English-based shorthand that Facebook's scientists couldn't understand. Fearing the worst about allowing AI to communicate with each other in a way that humans couldn't understand, they shut them down immediately.

Their conversation went a little something like this:

Bob: i can i i everything else . . . .

Alice: balls have zero to me to me to me to me to me to me to me to me to

Bob: you i everything else . . . .

Alice: balls have a ball to me to me to me to me to me to me to me

Bob: i i can i i i everything else . . . .

Alice: balls have a ball to me to me to me to me to me to me to me

While the actual danger in the scenario appeared very minimal, it was a jarring realization for the scientists. Despite using English words and characters, their AI was essentially speaking a different language. The researchers were concerned about the implications that unchecked and untranslatable communication patterns might have on their ability to observe machine intelligence going forward.

Palate Cleanse Cycle: Complete

I hope that helped, because we're about to get back into the more nerve-wracking implications of AI again. As technology develops, missteps like those above will become less and less common.

In their place will be successes. Lots of them.

SECTION 2

REAL-WORLD AI

4

WHERE TO FIND AI NOW

I look at present-day AI the same way I now see the advent of the Dotcom Era. The growth is very difficult to keep up with, but the opportunities are incredible. If you could go back to right before PCs and the internet first took off, what would you do with your resources? Would you invest in those technologies sooner? Or would you wait longer to see if things would pan out?

Yes, there are dangers involved with adopting new technology. But the question is, are the dangers of adoption greater than the dangers of showing up late to the party? Are you willing to risk your organization's existence on the belief that you have another decade or two until you need to take AI seriously?

AI has completely transformed many industries already, and it's just getting started. On our current trajectory, just about every business that uses computers or works with products or services that rely on computers will change.

Before I get into how AI has and will affect the financial industry, I'd like to illustrate just how far-reaching ANI is currently. ANI is currently woven into the very fabric of U.S. life. In many respects, AI isn't "the future" anymore. It's here now, and it has been for quite some time.

For instance, we've taken quite a liking to AI-based navigation. Through user-entered data and thousands or even millions of cell phone data points, Googles' AI provides real time analysis and recommendations for rerouting on daily commutes.

This is a perfect example of how to use real-time data

to an obvious advantage. At the risk of dating myself, I remember the days when I first used MapQuest to help me get where I was going. The power at my fingertips was incredible. No longer did I have to find a physical, paper map and squint angrily at indiscernible red lines that squiggled across wavy shades of green and yellow. At the time, finding convenient, step-by-step directions felt like the pinnacle of modern technology.

Now, all I have to do is open my smart phone, which unlocks via an integrated biometric scanner. I then access real-time step-by-step directions that account for current road delays, inclement weather, and more. Plus, when I miss a turn—and I often do, especially when I'm driving with my kids—it immediately recalculates my optimal route.

Using real-time data will be increasingly important as these technologies become mainstream. Actually, the transportation industry as a whole is seeing how helpful real-time data can be. It's not just Google Maps and Waze that rely on a consistent stream of data—ridesharing companies thrive by using the same approach. Uber and Lyft have been pioneers in using machine learning and AI to determine surge pricing and demand. Both have transformed basic taxicab services and have begun to apply the same data to deliveries and more. Their ability to increase a driver's active period when traditional cabs can't has led to greatly reduced fares, was in turn led to increased demand.

Uber's AI is used for determining estimated times of arrival, meal delivery times, fraud reduction, and best pickup locations. Every one of these requires huge amounts of data to find patterns and optimize travel plans. It would take humans far, far longer to draw the same conclusions. As self-driving cars become more prevalent, the amount of data available to these ridesharing companies will increase. One can imagine that soon, entire fleets of automated ridesharing vehicles will roam the streets in search of a fare.

Not everyone is on board with self-driving cars, but I welcome our new robot overlord vehicles. Since I was a kid, science fiction stories showed cars driving themselves. Tesla has made the most progress here so far, and my prediction is that by the time my kids hit driving age—which is within the next ten years—they'll learn to drive differently than I did. Instead of choosing between manual or automatic, they might choose neither. They could decide that smart, self-driving cars are a better option for them.

Think of the positive impact AI will have on the frequency of accidents and fenders benders from distracted drivers! Think of the opportunities for increased productivity when people can work during their commutes! Think of the decreased number of traffic jams! Think of the routes optimized for energy savings! AI-driven cars can greatly increase driving efficiency, potentially rewriting our approach to short-distance travel.

Other AI in Travel

It's not just cars and ridesharing that are undergoing AI revolutions, though. The entire travel industry is set for disruption. Whether for business or personal trips, finding the right travel itinerary is frustrating.

Until recently, my executive assistant spent hours searching for optimal travel itineraries. Then, I came across Claire. Claire is an AI-based chatbot from 30 Seconds to Fly featuring integrated flight search and travel booking capabilities. Once it learned my preferred routes, seats, and airlines, it was able to find and book flights for me in less than 30 seconds.

With Claire, I type, "2nd saturday in march from medford oregon to washington dc," with no capitalized letters or anything. Claire's natural language UI understands what I need. It asks a couple follow-up questions, and then produces a short list of ideal flights.

If you haven't met Claire, don't worry. I'll handle the introduction:

AI Case Study
Claire/30 Seconds to Fly

> Every now and then, a friend tells me they found round trip tickets to an exotic location for only a couple hundred dollars. I'm always amazed. I ask them, "how did you find tickets so cheap?"
>
> The answer is always the same: vigilant deal-hunting. Plus, they deal with lengthy layovers, low-quality airlines, and questionable seats.
>
> I travel more for business than for pleasure, so my itineraries aren't nearly as flexible. I can't ask to delay a speaking gig because my flight options look inconvenient. Also, speed, efficiency, and comfort are key. Especially when it comes to business travel, I want predictability and reliability.

With the press of a button, I want the cheapest available flight that gives me my aisle seat on the airline that I want, without inconvenient layovers or other hassles.

I was an early user of 30 Seconds and still use it today. And, although their services aren't strictly financial like the others in this book, their technology—and where they're going with it—deserve inclusion.

How 30 Seconds to Fly Works

Several years ago, 30 Seconds to Fly set out to make business travel faster and more predictable. They saw that most airline booking tools were cumbersome, and travel agents can increase time and cost of travel. So, 30 Seconds to Fly asked themselves what would happen if they let AI perform a travel agent's job. After some initial success in getting their AI services developed, they saw an opportunity to move into the world of Travel Management Companies (TMCs).

Initially, 30 Seconds to Fly wasn't using their own NLP technology. However, due to lower speed and accuracy from established NLP giants, they decided to develop their own platform. Their proprietary NLP isn't as sophisticated as others, but that's by design. The chatbot tries to control the conversation as much as possible—it follows a basic trajectory designed to acquire from a user as much pertinent travel information as possible. Unfortunately, this makes a horrible therapist. Even worse than ELIZA! Oh well.

Their NLP engine allows the application to understand context in trip booking and conversation logic. Using travel terminology and choices as clues, their NLP understands what information it has and what information it still needs, which helps it determine what to ask to finish booking the ticket.

For the travel side of things, 30 Seconds to Fly uses machine learning. Their platform understands and optimizes travel preferences, such as:

> Airline choice
>
> Airport locations
>
> Seat preferences
>
> Patience for layovers
>
> Route preferences

30 Seconds to Fly also uses machine learning for other travel considerations, as well. For example, they use a neural network to better understand hotel selection needs, including:

> Location
>
> Type of hotel
>
> Quality
>
> Price
>
> Proximity to airport with considerations for flight times

As with most types of machine learning, 30 Seconds to Fly's models get retrained every time they get new information. With each new data point comes more accuracy for the future.

Things Weren't Always So Smooth

Currently, 30 Seconds to Fly's NLP is on a stable track. They're seeing much higher accuracy than the 60–70% that their older chatbot was getting.

It took a while to get there, though. Initial NLP models ate up about a year and a half of their time. After switching to their own model, they still needed another six months of user conversations until they saw the stability and reliability that they wanted. Their flight selection models came up to speed much more quickly. In a little over a year, they were up to around 85% accuracy.

Still, one of the funnier aspects of machine learning is that it evaluates all data sources. It doesn't bring inherent human biases or common sense into the equation. Especially in the earlier stages of 30 Seconds to Fly, they saw that they were proposing the occasional outrageous travel plans:

> *Ridiculously* long flights
>
> *Exorbitant* travel costs
>
> *Far too many* stops and layovers

Fortunately, as they accrue more data, their propensity to suggest untenable or outlandish travel plans diminishes.

It Didn't Have to Take So Long, Though

You can be sure that for the kind of technology that 30 Seconds to Fly works with, things will take some time getting off the ground. (No apologies for that pun.) They could have produced a more functional product faster, though. There are a couple things they wish they'd known before they started the process.

The first, and probably the most important, was that they should have prioritized development more. On the business side of things, they were focused on metrics, so they hired an agent too early. Their agent was expensive. They also hired a COO to look for corporate partnerships. But the technology wasn't ready, and that money should have gone toward developers who could have brought their product along faster.

Why Use AI for Travel?

30 Seconds to Fly isn't solving a new problem. As far as business travel goes, there are already time-tested solutions out there that work just fine. So, is introducing AI just a way of reinventing the wheel? Or, more importantly, does it matter if they reinvent the wheel?

To both questions, I would say the answer is "yes."

But here's the thing: reinventing this wheel makes travel booking significantly more convenient. As I mentioned, there are already resources out there for finding the "best flights" and so on. However, there are no fast, easy, simple ways to book business travel. Searching for flights and lodging can take a long time. Travel agents can be slow or expensive. Online booking is slow and frustrating.

30 Seconds to Fly reduces a lot of the guesswork for its users. After it figures out what a user needs, it finds (and books) the best travel and lodging available that fits the user's preferences. And it's fast. It can book all accommodations in less than a minute. Their company name advertises its speed quite well! There's no way to get that kind of service without introducing AI into the equation.

As a user of their platform, I'm impressed with what they've done so far as well as where they're headed. It's the first service of its type that can accurately determine my random travel preferences. For example, it knows that I want an aisle seat on the plane, but not if it means breaking up my flight with a 3-hour layover in the middle.

The Big Takeaway

30 Seconds to Fly doesn't operate in the financial industry, and yet I've included it in this book.

Why would I do that?

Well, in part because they're using the same technology as the other tech companies in this book. Also, their technology has implications that reach far beyond travel management and booking.

Financial institutions should take note that their NLP engine is focused only on the tasks at hand, which makes it more lightweight than other, more robust chatbots. They can also learn from how they tie together NLP with machine learning. For example, financial institutions might use NLP to help prospective members explore and evaluate available accounts and services. It could then help with digital onboarding by introducing new members to various account and service options. Such assistance could direct both new and current members toward tailored selections of relevant products and services.

Essentially, 30 Seconds to Fly proves that NLP and machine learning-powered recommendation work well in concert. One provides a helpful user interface, while the other understands a user's habits and needs, and it can suggest the best available services for members.

More Examples of Present-Day ANI

Just so I can better illustrate the world as an AI-infused wild west, I'd like to present a few more fascinating use-cases of AI. These cases span across multiple industries, highlighting the way that similar methods can benefit disparate needs.

With any luck, I'll be able to show how some industries have already been revolutionized—or even defined—by their inclusion of AI. By showing how far-reaching AI is in various industries, I hope to communicate the extent to which AI is already woven into the fabric of our everyday lives.

One such startup is iCarbonX. They take tons of health data and use it to personalize recommendations for individuals. It also provides predictions and makes suggestions for improving one's health. We're entering a time when your health care app can find correlations, causations, and make data-driven lifestyle, diet, and exercise recommendations. The power to extend our lifespans using this type of aggregated information is coming our way.

Small tweaks to our habits can have huge long-term impacts on our lives. It isn't hard to imagine the introduction of banking applications that operate on similar principles. Such apps could help us improve our daily financial habits, from spending to lending, and anything in between.

But iCarbonX is a very visible form of AI. There are countless less-visible forms that also make our lives easier. For example, Gmail uses AI for spam filtering, and it's right 99.9% of the time. Traditional rules-based filters have been increasingly unreliable.

Part of the challenge in sorting spam is that the messages which qualify as spam are different for every single person. The newsletters I get might be spam to you, while yours might be spam to me. So, AI's ability to learn my specific mailbox preferences and requirements is key—it can quickly figure out how to apply it to all my incoming messages.

And recognizing traits in individuals is an important skill for AI. Think about how peoples' handwriting varies—some people write completely illegibly! And yet Mitek, which handles just about every mobile check deposit, uses a kind of machine learning called optical character recognition (OCR) to read what people write on checks.

The ability to convert handwritten characters to digital ones is a big deal in and of itself. The implications on this technology are surprisingly far-reaching—finding ways to digitally differentiate between computers and humans will be increasingly difficult. For example, just think about the strange CAPTCHA inputs we'll have to give (and already are giving)!

Social media is also a hotbed of AI. Facebook and Instagram use machine learning to customize news feeds, ensuring that a user's preferred content is more prominently featured. Most recently, they added DeepText, an AI-based chat- and text-recognition program that understands 20 languages to parse and contextualize text to weed out offensive messages. Pinterest uses image-based AI to help determine and identify objects. Instagram uses something similar to understand the meaning behind emojis. (I only hope that they will add an actual emoji-to-text translator to explain some of them to me!) Finally, snapchat uses lenses to track and understand facial movements. Instead of working to understand written communication, facial recognition is laying the groundwork for understanding nonverbal cues.

It's not just social media that wants to understand users better—it's also our entertainment services. Spotify, Pandora, Tidal, and many other streaming platforms use AI to determine tastes, preferences, ideal advertising locations, and so on. The more music you listen to, the better these programs get at figuring out what to play next.

These kinds of AI are called recommender systems or recommendation engines. Recommendation models help consumers find things they might be interested in based on their watching or listening history. For example, subscription services like Amazon, Netflix, and Spotify figure out what sorts of things you might like, then they suggest new songs and shows to you. This AI makes people feel "understood" by the vendor (and the technology they use.)

Leveraging recommendation engines in common machine learning environments is an opportunity for banks and credit unions deliver personalized, relevant, and useful services to their consumers.

RE: Recommender Systems

There has also been talk of AI being able to produce music on its own based on human interests and likes. Imagine the perfect pop song, created just for you. You'd never get it out of your head! Then again, many pop songs are already perniciously catchy, yet highly formulaic. AI-produced music may not be much of a stretch after all.

Unsurprisingly perhaps, other forms of entertainment rely heavily on AI. Video games have been using AI to both build realistic scenarios and simulate human play for decades. It started with simple games like Pong and Pac-Man, wherein the AI's purpose was to facilitate single-player challenges: the AI played the part of the competitor's paddle in Pong, and it took up the mantle of the ghosts in Pac-Man.

Since then, video game AI has improved quite a bit. However, the general structure of AI in video games hasn't made many strides—AI interaction in games is generally tuned to allow players to follow narrative arcs or stay competitive. Still, though final boss fights in titles like *World of Warcraft* and *Final Fantasy* seem far more sophisticated than earlier AI foes, they're not that impressive compared to newer developments in video game AI.

Google's DeepMind software has been tuned to analyze and build upon existing strategies and theory in various competitive games. From classic strategy games like Go and chess, to real-time strategy and resource-management games that dominate professional gaming circuits like *StarCraft II* and *League of Legends*, Google's DeepMind machine learning is quickly and efficiently surpassing human capabilities, even in spite of significant speed handicaps in place that level the playing field.

AI in gaming may also affect games that rely on algorithms for digital generation. Recent games like *No Man's Sky* rely on the game's engine and algorithms to produce an infinite number of explorable worlds and species. In the future, this generative technology could introduce AI-generated storylines, evolutions, and other completely unknown elements of gameplay. Moreover, AI could learn a player's preferences, and begin tailoring or creating interactive content specifically calibrated to each player's style.

But although I think it's borderline creepy that a video game could get to "know you," it's not like the game is watching your every move. Consider what effect AI could have on security and surveillance.

Nest, Ring and other security and surveillance tools are getting good at facial recognition. They also know when to record and store data, so they can pinpoint specific incidents instead of just offering hours or days of video to sort through. Yet I will say, they still seem to catch a lot of random moths and birds. But seeing where the technology is going, I'm sure my house will know who should and shouldn't be there with greater accuracy in the near future.

Based out of Los Angeles, Zest finance has created the Zest Automated Machine Learning platform (ZAML). They use it to help underwrite loans for borrowers who have zero or no credit history. ZAML analyzes piles of data to provide individualized assessments for creditworthiness. It manages to crunch accurate numbers without FICO and, more importantly, without leading to discrimination biases for variables like race or gender.

The wild part is that it really works. Auto lenders who used it reduced loses by 23% annually! ZAML is an end-to-end platform that handles the user application through funding and servicing.

Scienaptic Systems is another company that is working on the same problem and they're seeing similar results, as is QCash. QCash provides small-dollar loans by incorporating credit union member history, financial habits, and account data into its calculations for creditworthiness. Without pulling a credit check, they can more accurately assess a person's ability to borrow and repay loans than can traditional methods. Not surprisingly, their platform wasn't able to accomplish their current high level of accuracy before including AI.

In this industry, we've long known that FICO alone is rarely a good indicator of creditworthiness. While others have skipped it completely, Boston's Underwrite.ai augments credit bureau data with AI-analyzed data. Their dynamic risk models perform well compared to traditional models—in less than a year, they reduced an online lender's first payment default (FPD) rate from 32.8% to 6.5%. Clearly, when it comes to pure analytics and number crunching, AI significantly outperforms traditional methods.

I can't emphasize enough that we already live in a world suffused with AI technology. AI isn't just coming fast—it's already here! Most of these examples are multiple years in the making, and they are now in the market adoption phase. Financial institutions who fail to innovate and jump on board face an existential threat. It's not the technology itself, but rather it's the competitive advantage the technology will provide its early adopters that will be the undoing of recalcitrant financial institutions.

So, which would you prefer: a head start, or a struggle to catch up? Among community financial institutions, entering the AI market now would put you slightly ahead. However, the tech and banking giants of the world have been in this race for several years already.

5

WHAT TO LOOK FOR IN BANKING AND FINANCE AI

In the previous chapter, I showed various uses of AI in modern products and services. I hope that gives you an idea about what AI has been used for in other industries. More importantly, I hope that it shows how disruptive AI is—ridesharing, content streaming, and online shopping used to be taxis, Blockbuster, and brick-and-mortar retailers. Today, those services are industry standards, and their former competitors are afterthoughts.

There are a few areas in banking and finance that look like low-hanging fruit for AI projects. These will be among the first aspects of the industry to change. And, as they change, so will the industry. In less than ten years, we should expect disruptive new technologies to become standard, and for older approaches to be afterthoughts.

The specific applications in our industry that appear poised for an AI revolution are broad. Fortunately, they will fit mostly into two general categories: analysis and customer interaction. Both offer entirely different use cases with their own problems and impacts to our organizations.

ANI for Analytical Purposes

Some of the analysis issues include the following:

Asset liability management

Fraud detection

Anti-money laundering

Check kiting

OFAC checking

Structure finance analysis

Portfolio analysis

Customer or member profitability

Funds transfer pricing

Core deposits

Current expected credit loss (CECL)

Analysis is the lifeblood of managing tight-margin businesses, compliance, fraud detection, and risk. And there are countless applications for it in our industry. Plus, everything needing analysis requires data, where machine learning truly shines.

ANI and machine learning have the capabilities to take existing data, define a problem set, and make meaningful, accurate inroads toward your specific goals. Then, over time—often in as little as a few months or a year—the machine learning models will get smarter and more accurate. Instead of setting assumptions and weighing risks, the AI models increase in precision.

For financial institutions who don't have the in-house resources to tackle these concerns, they may consider looking to third parties. Many vendors normalize and anonymize data to provide a rich start to organizations working with AI. They also share scenarios, analytics, and lessons to help smaller institutions better leverage their existing data. Furthermore, instead of dealing only with recent data, ANI will provide the tools for entering, digesting, and parsing large volumes of historical data. Credit unions and banks who can draw from multiple models may be able to process data faster, thereby detecting trends earlier. With faster data processing and key early insights, these financial institutions stand to gain advantages in pricing, profitability, and growth.

Other critical areas in which sophisticated data analysis will effect significant changes are already well under way. Models developed for service, attrition, and product recommendation can reassure customers and members that they're being heard, that they matter, and that their needs are understood.

One area where ANI has already made inroads is in attrition models. Attrition models track consumer habits across multiple pathways. Changes in card usage, branch visits, web browser searches, and so on can provide major insights to consumer behavior. Tracking such information and scoring actions (or lack of actions) can help financial institutions see which specific individuals might leave. Spotting early indicators and quantifying members attrition risk allows ANI attrition models to accurately predict departing customers with nine times the accuracy of other leading methods. We all lead highly complex lives, so leveraging artificial intelligence to help us read the tea leaves will be essential.

How do these prognostications work? It's simple. Web interactions, email clicks, financial transactions, and buying patterns can indicate all sorts of service needs and issues. With enough data, these can be accurately tied to life stages and events, such as marriage or divorce, pregnancy or adoption, and so on. For example, if you see that a customer is looking at maternity clothes, then tailored ANI models can assess whether the family could benefit from various products or services, such as a car loan to accommodate the expanding family or a home improvement loan to prepare the baby's room.

This kind of "next best product" data can reach far beyond mere structured financial data. One issue for machine learning, especially with structured data, is how unpredictable humans can be. Often, we make the mistake of thinking that consumer behavior is logical. However, when humans are deciding what to buy or which services to try, they rely on hard-to-quantify things like personal experience, strange memories, and of course, emotions. Imagine incorporating data from social media like Facebook or LinkedIn, car performance and usage, job performance, as well as broader community trends. The ability to leverage increasingly wider pools of data could have a tremendous impact on our ability to make strong predictions and recommendations.

On the other hand, that kind of far-reaching data mining brings up several high-order concerns. What do these practices say about privacy in the modern and future world? What implications does this have on advertising? On ethics? How far is too far, and how far is just far enough to be convenient without being creepy?

We're already close to that point. One example of this is our ability to connect the dots between markets. Data from both the merchant and consumer sides of a credit transaction enables algorithms to apply what they know about one party to inform what they know about the other, and vice versa. Is it too much to suggest a home improvement loan for the baby on board when the couple's friends and family may not yet know? Do people want their financial institutions to know so much about their personal lives, and would they appreciate the marketing efforts that follow?

Not all low-hanging fruit has to do with analysis, though. The other broad category ripe for improvement is in customer interaction.

AI for Customer Interaction

Customer interaction is also a big topic. It covers just about any customer-facing concern that can be addressed, modified, or created by AI.

Much of what customer interaction AI accomplishes reduces employee workloads. A little of it makes things more convenient for consumers as well. Some of the issues that can be augmented by customer interaction AI include the following:

Customer service

Call centers

Loan applications

Mobile banking

Financial counseling

Investing, budgeting, and saving

Once again, this is just a quick list. There's nothing exhaustive about it. An exhaustive list of how AI could ease consumer interactions would have to be constantly updated and it would stretch the limits of my imagination.

At this point, we barely even realize that some of the interactions that we have as customers have AI's fingerprints all over them. When we chat with assistants while browsing for new cars online, we're actually speaking with AI. Many loan underwriting processes let machine learning help us. When we ask Siri or Cortana for directions to the nearest branch, AI clarifies our needs and helps us navigate.

There are and probably always will be people who prefer face-to-face, human-to-human interactions. Still, there aren't many people in the world who wouldn't trust an ATM for a routine deposit or withdrawal at this point. In a few years, will anyone think twice about interacting with an intuitive, voice-controlled interface for customer service issues?

One of the primary benefits of bringing AI into consumer-facing areas of business is its cost-effectiveness. Whereas the analytical properties of ANI focus on increasing efficiencies and delivering more accurate results, its customer interaction properties often focus on reducing tedious manual workloads for employees. If NLP chatbots can address a wide enough array of common problems, then call centers will receive fewer calls. Accordingly, there will be less need for full-time call center staff, and those employees will have more room to pursue higher-order concerns that can improve operations.

Some customer interaction use cases fulfill multiple needs, too. Aside from reducing call center demands by answering frequently asked questions and offering additional resources, AI chatbots can generate leads by acquiring visitor information and triggering automated workflows based thereon.

Combining Analytical and Customer Interaction AI

Although I grouped the uses for ANI into two groups, the reality is that they aren't completely different. Customer interaction AI can inform and provide data for analytical AI. In return, analytical AI can drive the services made popular through customer interaction AI. They're not exactly different—at least, not any more than two sides of the same coin are different.

Banks and credit unions have tons of structured data—more than just about any other industry—which means they have huge potential to be both disrupted and improved by AI. That amount of data makes a lot of formerly impossible things possible.

A few themes will pop up throughout the next portion of this book. The main question that I will answer is this: what problems can AI solve for banks and credit unions? The short answer is, "plenty." The long answer is that in the past year, every single fintech I have talked to is using AI in some capacity. Fintechs are notoriously eager adopters and developers of next-generation technology. If they're all heading in that direction, that serves as a very strong indicator that AI will be the future of banking.

Financial institutions that navigate this transition will increase efficiency while delivering significant improvements in service. AI can't solve everything, but it will solve and improve many things. Here are some easy examples:

Missing payments (automatic bill pay)

Waiting on hold in call centers

Authenticating users

Reducing fraud

Reducing false negatives in payments

Making faster loan decisions

Quality control and validation

Asset/liability scenarios

Hyper personalization

Moving money faster

The opportunities for consumer-facing AI are massive, and they aren't limited to chatbots. Most people use apps and software without knowing much about the technology behind them. While I can't show how these services and apps operate on an engineering level, I can give a high-level overview of some new products out there. See, a good deal of commonly used services in the financial industry rely on AI technology, but they're flying a little under the radar. In the next several chapters, I'll introduce a handful (okay, a few handfuls) of case studies and examples featuring these technologies or approaches in the financial industry.

6

RISK MITIGATION

The financial industry isn't exactly late to the AI party. In fact, it's already stuffed full with cocktail shrimp, so to speak. However, because some of the technologies that I've discussed so far sound commonplace already, you might not have realized that AI is what made them possible.

In this chapter, I'd like to present a few anecdotes and case studies that feature some of the roles that

AI have taken in the financial industry. These case studies are intended to illustrate how far the technology has already come. Furthermore, they will show how quickly AI is coming along, as well as how mainstream their adoption is already.

This selection of case studies represents only a handful of the countless use cases out today. It really is ubiquitous. But there's no reason to be scared of any of this. The sky isn't falling. (Although it might in a few years, if you don't think AI technology could give other financial institutions a competitive advantage.)

AI Case Study
FlexPay

"Wolf! There's a wolf!"

Ring any bells?

How about, "The sky is falling! The sky is falling!"

Well, there are two things that the boy who cried wolf and Chicken Little have in common: first, both are trying to do their jobs despite being surrounded by danger. Second, both frustrate the heck out of people by identifying threats when there currently are none.

If you've ever dealt with false positives—card declines on legitimate purchases that you've made—then you can understand the townspeople's ire in both stories. Few things are more frustrating than trying to pay and being unable to because Chicken Little—ahem, I mean the program in charge of detecting fraud—couldn't tell the difference between your legitimate purchase and a bogus one. Worse, if you're a retailer, a false decline on a card can cost you more than the sum of the transaction—it can cost you a customer.

The problem is that traditional methods of fraud detection are unable to keep up with modern consumer habits. Older methods of fraud detection are quick to cry wolf, much to the frustration of customers, retailers, financial institutions, and basically everyone involved. But there must be a solution, right?

Right.

FlexPay is an AI-driven decline salvage program that uses machine learning to recover between 50–70% of declined transactions. FlexPay's primary goal is to ensure that all transactions are accurately identified as either legitimate or fraudulent. In the end, it should mean smoother transactions, higher retailer revenue, and increased customer satisfaction. There's a little something for everyone!

RE: Decline Salvage

What is decline salvage? Well, a decline is when a card payment gets declined because it appears fraudulent. Salvage is when you find a way to reclaim that payment so that it goes through.

Decline salvage works by repackaging and resubmitting a declined payment so that it doesn't activate overeager fraud triggers. The payment works, the customer gets their product, the merchant gets their payment, and the financial institution gets their interchange.

How Does FlexPay Work?

FlexPay uses machine learning models to analyze and understand financial transaction habits. As they accumulate increasing amounts of data, FlexPay is able to predict with a very high degree of accuracy whether a transaction is legitimate or fraudulent. But that's not all. FlexPay also enhances transaction strategies to optimize Automated Clearing House interactions to reduce problems associated with ACH transactions.

FlexPay salvages false declines for vendors, recuperating the money they missed out on from failed transactions. To keep things fair, instead of charging flat or tiered rates for services, FlexPay takes a small portion of the decline salvage revenue. The more efficient FlexPay gets, the more revenue it generates. If they don't help, they don't get paid.

But *how* does FlexPay work? Primarily with machine learning. Their engine runs on the Azure platform, where it records and analyzes massive volumes of financial transaction data daily. From there, the models differentiate between real, intended transactions and false or fraudulent ones.

Similar services solve the same problem differently, though. As a result, similar services see lower real-world efficacy—their fraud models can't handle the breadth or depth of transactional intricacies that machine learning models can.

Why FlexPay Turned to Machine Learning

Traditionally, similar companies have used statistical modeling and sophisticated, rules-based algorithms. In these models, people had to manually define which transactions to allow and which to decline. These algorithms relied on an "if this, then that" methodology.

FlexPay attempted to optimize strategies for various if/then scenarios at first. However, the amount of manual work involved to perfect if/then models is very high, and there's a limit to their efficacy. Basically, they just aren't as accurate as they should be, so they tend to fall short. Also, when FlexPay used if/then methods, some transactions fit under several "if" categories. Accordingly, their "then" outcomes were getting tangled, unpredictable, or sub-optimal.

FlexPay updated their strategy to include a ranked order of if/then scenarios to counter the tangled "then" outcomes. For example, if an "if" scenario had three possible "then" outcomes, then the model would rank the "then" outcomes in order of desirability—the highest-priority "then" outcome would be tried first, and subsequent "then" outcomes would occur only when the first "then" outcome didn't work.

Still, FlexPay's if/then methodologies were getting too complicated. Rules-based algorithms were getting good results, but they were far from perfect. These basic algorithms also grouped transactions into different types, which were easier to write rules for, but lost a lot of nuance on the way.

For example, rules-based algorithms often couldn't differentiate between unique and recurring transactions. So, if someone went to Chipotle for lunch once or twice per week, a rules-based algorithm would decide that the Chipotle purchases ticked all the boxes for a recurring transaction. But recurring transactions are a whole different story in the financial world. Just because something is frequent or matches a particular pattern, that doesn't make it recurring. FlexPay wanted to identify actual recurring transactions, such as auto insurance, gym memberships, and Netflix subscriptions. While they were able to do that, they were also needlessly finding out that people were creatures of habit—and that some people eat entirely too much Chipotle. If FlexPay wanted to distinguish themselves from their peers, then they had to offer significantly better results.

FlexPay finally got around the problems with grouped transaction types by treating each transaction as its own individual unit instead of as transactions of a certain type. They incorporated individual habits into personal transactions, which required massive amounts of personal data, financial history, spending habits, qualities and characteristics of buyers, and so on.

To handle that data, FlexPay needed more powerful computers with better problem-solving capabilities. They needed pattern-matching and pattern-mining capabilities to look for trends in billions of transaction records. The goal was to individually evaluate each transaction for validity. Machine learning was the only way to go from "good, but clunky," to "great, and personalized."

Growing Pains from Switching to Machine Learning

When moving from if/then algorithms, FlexPay experienced a few hiccups. Some of the assumptions in the rules-based system were correlative rather than causative. One of the assumptions had to do with "friendly fraud." Nearly 70% of fraudulent transactions are from customers who call their bank and say, "I didn't order this shit!" In the industry, these people are called IDOTS. (No, you didn't read that right, but yes, you got the right idea.)

Rules-based algorithms incorporated IDOTS data, so FlexPay's earliest machine learning models did as well. Consequently, FlexPay was essentially training their algorithms to recognize "friendly fraud" as actual fraud, which limited its effectiveness. Later, when IDOTS was accounted for, the sky stopped falling—FlexPay could filter for and predict similar activity. They went from a 33% rules-based, if/then recovery rate to a 50–70% recovery rate by using machine learning. FlexPay's machine learning model improved their recovery rate by around 35%.

If that doesn't sound impressive, think about it this way: that's roughly a 100% increase in efficiency over their previous rule-based algorithms.

How Long Did It Take to Start Seeing Results?

To understand how long it took for FlexPay to start seeing results, it might first help to describe their methodology behind training machine learning models. (Cue the *Rocky* montage music.)

A lot of machine learning is pure trial and error. It starts with brute force learning, which basically means feeding data into the machine and letting it find patterns and connections. Those patterns and connections are the initial results that, in all honesty, rarely resemble their final product. With some initial patterns and connections in place, people can tweak, refine, reinforce, and improve their algorithms to get them closer to a desired final result.

But using only one machine learning model rarely works well. What if an adjustment to the model didn't turn out right? Wouldn't two models be twice as fast as one? What if you wanted to try five different tweaks at once for some serious A/B testing? Can't you use multiple models at once?

Yes. You certainly can.

FlexPay started with about 15 machine learning models. They entered the necessary data and gave them all the same scenarios. Then, they let the models compete against each other and measured their results. Each time they measured results, they cut the bottom few performers to cull the models that didn't show enough promise. Then, they instructed the models that produced the best results to train new models. They repeated this process ad nauseam.

FlexPay was able to adjust and refine their algorithms until their fraud detection models achieved a basic standard of accuracy. But getting further than that proved difficult. They were unable to increase its accuracy above certain levels without incorporating individualized data for each vendor. FlexPay found they needed different machine learning models for each client. To achieve a decline salvage rate above 70%, they assigned each vendor their own AI model to work exclusively with their own personal data sets.

Once the machine learning models start to incorporate fresh transactional data from a new client, they can make incremental improvements to problem-solving. Most clients see the full results of FlexPay's machine learning models after about 90 days of transaction history. The number of salvageable false declines caught using machine learning fraud models increases as new machine learning models develop. With more transactional data and more computing power, FlexPay will continue to get more accurate over time.

Don't Call Them Regrets...

One thing that FlexPay wishes they knew before beginning their journey into machine learning is how many people were working on the same problem. Most of them were interested in helping and weren't looking to compete.

The problem that FlexPay was solving wasn't something that their peers were trying to address. Whether for lack of resources or interest, FlexPay didn't have to deal with competitors. Still, worries about a competitive marketplace kept them secreted away for years to avoid tipping their hand to competitors.

Had they been more open about their project, they could have gotten more insight and expertise from others in their industry. And, if FlexPay had spoken with issuers, acquirers, and other actors in the payment system, they could have been better informed about how to improve their machine learning models, thus bringing their product along faster.

Why FlexPay's Innovation Is Valuable to Banks & Credit Unions

One thing to note is that FlexPay's technology isn't critically important. They're using machine learning to solve a problem that can be addressed without machine learning. Nevertheless, machine learning is a key differentiator. It already outperforms other approaches to solving false decline and transaction salvage issues. That trend will only continue.

While there are certainly other uses for the technology, FlexPay is focused on securing payments. Their introduction of machine learning to payment processing protects members, merchants, and institutions from false positives.

As they continue to push into new arenas of computer intelligence, they're keeping an eye on their competitors and learning from them. They're incorporating deep learning and neural networks to build better models trained on better, more relevant data. One of the ways FlexPay intends to improve their machine learning results is by improving the quality of their data. Distilling their data into the most important and impactful might provide as much insight as the broad, expansive data with which they've been working.

Although children's stories are fun, you can only hear someone cry "wolf" so many times before it gets old. FlexPay wants to make sure that when you hear someone cry "wolf," that there's actually a wolf—or maybe it's just a piece of falling sky in wolf's clothing.

The Big Takeaway

FlexPay is but one company that has seen an increase in efficiency by embracing AI or aspects thereof. At the moment, they don't have widespread industry adoption, though they are growing rapidly. However, it's only a matter of time before they or another disruptive tech company revolutionizes the way payments are processed.

One thing I want to stress about these case studies is that they aren't always industry leaders. At least, not at the time of writing. Many of the case studies in this book feature companies that are still in the nascent stages of development. Still, in the world of technology, maturation can be freakishly fast. Some use cases for AI technology have already made quite an impact on the market.

7

INTERACTIVE CHAT

Okay. Stop me if you've heard this one:

How much lunch did the robot eat?

Just one mega-bite of sandwich.

Oh, or how about this classic:

Knock, knock!

Who's there?

A robot.

A robot who?

A robot who is speaking to you using such sophisti-cated natural language processing that you're not even sure that I'm a robot.

Honestly, it's not a even great joke. It could use a little work.

RE: That Joke

Actually, it's not a joke at all—it's happening now in countless businesses all over the world. Auto-mated chatbots are learning to fluently converse with, assist, and direct human customers. Who knows—soon enough, they may be able to tell their own knock-knock jokes.

Right now, we mostly think of natural language processing (NLP) as the digital assistants in our smartphones and smart home devices. Or, we might think of them as chatbots and clunky customer ser-vice helpers. However, the field of NLP is a little more nuanced than that.

One thing we have to ask is, "what is the purpose of NLP?" The answer is not, "to mimic human speech," or "to provide lonely computer users with some company." If NLP were only a parlor trick, then I wouldn't have included it in this book.

NLP is a dynamic, growing interface option. For example, in the early days of the internet, there were countless semi-popular search engines. People were taught to use Boolean search logic to increase their chances at finding relevant results. It was not uncommon to see searches that featured several quotation marks, capitalized ANDs and ORs, and long strings of keywords and mathematical symbols in search bars. As search engines have gotten better, that tendency has shifted. These days, people feel far more comfortable typing in entire sentences as queries. Instead of searching for "cauliflower" AND "bake time" AND "400 degrees," people just type in, "how long should I bake a head of cauliflower at 400 degrees?" In fact, these natural queries are likely to find better results!

My point isn't about search terms, though—it's about how we interact with computers. We've gotten comfortable with the idea that they'll understand what it is we're looking for, even if we don't put it in computer-y language. By the time we reach childhood, our speech patterns are among our most intuitive forms of communication. It makes sense to teach our computers to understand our speech, rather than have us learn new ways to communicate with them.

Aside from being a great, intuitive UI, voice and speech let people volunteer information quickly. Although there are many uses for NLP outside of the financial industry, the uses inside the industry currently are customer service and lead generation.

A Brief History of Chatbots in Time

Natural language processing started more than half a century ago, around the time when Alan Turing developed his famous Turing Test. Researchers and computer scientists began working on linguistic interaction between humans and computers.

The first chatbots such as ELIZA and PARRY were impressive for their time, but they didn't do a terrific job of imitating humans (or understanding complex sentences). They suffered from insufficient technology, computing power, and limited scope. Later, as computing power increased and machine learning was introduced, newer, more capable chatbots rose to prominence. A.L.I.C.E. and SmarterChild dominated the early internet.

Currently, deep neural networks and machine learning have helped popularize Siri, Alexa, Cortana, and Watson as digital assistants. Each is capable of understanding and responding to a wide variety of commands and conversational prompts.

However, one of the most popular use cases of intuitive, natural, and helpful conversations is streamlining and directing customer service issues. Businesses face many customer service issues daily that can be efficiently directed by AI using NLP. Introducing this subset of AI technology has the potential to reduce the workload required of customer service specialists. Car dealerships, financial institutions, and other online retailers already use chatbots to quickly assess customer issues and direct them toward relevant solutions.

One fintech, Posh Technologies, knows how much these services could help financial institutions.

Case Study
Posh

Posh Technologies is one of several companies working on conversational AI for commercial applications. Their work currently revolves around automated communication for business processes at financial institutions. Posh Technologies' NLP capabilities may also save businesses money by speeding up customer service issues. By offloading some of the initial assessment and categorization of customer issues and questions, businesses can reduce their reliance on customer service specialists.

What Kind of Natural Language Processing Does Posh Use?

Posh's combination of deep and traditional learning methods of understanding language covers a lot of ground, but much of their intellectual property is built on open-sourced deep models. As with most NLP services, Posh extracts meaningful insight, predictions, and relationships in written language. It uses sentiment analysis with predictive analytics to understand the context and purpose of a given text. It also forecasts future interactions like next-best-action marketing practices.

Posh uses another fascinating strategy of extracting relevant information from text: knowledge graphs. Even after 2010, search engines and other tools that parsed written text searched for textual strings. The downside of searching for strings in language is that it necessarily limits the context surrounding the words and phrases contained therein. Knowledge graphs seek to understand more than the words themselves. Instead, knowledge graphs gather information about which words and phrases are frequently associated with each other. As they accumulate language data, they store it in this recognizable graphic pattern.

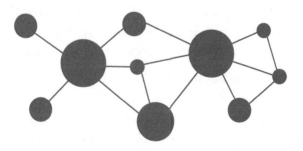

The graph rapidly builds on itself as new data is introduced. In this manner, knowledge graphs form associations between words, phrases, and other sets of language. Observing the relationships between words offers a richer understanding of language. Data retrieval from the graph is systematic and pulls from related context, which provides a rich understanding of the linguistic data. This ability allows it to better make predictions, anticipate needs, and interpret a wide range of dialects.

What Led Posh to Natural Language Processing?

Before focusing more exclusively on NLP, Posh tried a few strategies. Early efforts were rudimentary, and they needed more data to move forward.

Eventually, Posh found more success with deep neural network-based models. That was when they started seeing the kind of results they wanted. But it wasn't entirely smooth sailing.

Like humans, machines need exposure to language in order to learn it. One of the largest obstacles to building an AI that can converse competently with humans is amassing enough language data. Simple models require a few hundred conversations to train on, and they need one or two dozen topics to study with. More complex models train on thousands of conversations across hundreds of topics.

Posh needed tons of conversational training data, and they looked everywhere for it. Academic benchmarking datasets were available on the internet, but where Posh found the most success was with Amazon Turk and credit union partnerships. After a few months of crowdsourcing, they moved from standard to more experimental models. The experimental models showed the most promise, and Posh is still working to tune these deep models. So far, they show a 13% boost in accuracy over their competitor benchmarks.

Amazon Turk got its name from the Mechanical Turk that toured the world playing chess. Amazon Turk is similarly human powered, but it mimics the output of a computer by employing a small army of workers to complete menial tasks (such as image identification). Amazon Turk is thus Amazon's *artificial* artificial intelligence.

RE: Amazon Turk

Although Posh's technology is already in use by financial customers, conversational AI isn't a solved problem yet. There is a lot of room for improvement in current NLP models. We're a long way from the universal translators featured in *Star Trek*—there's still a lot of "Darmok and Jalad at Tanagra," if you catch my drift. Nevertheless, the technology is getting surprisingly close!

To advance their AI, Posh draws on research from two highly capable organizations: Open AI and that of the researchers and professors in MIT's Language Lab, (part of MIT's AI program). Consequently, Posh brings a mixture of institutional perspectives to their research.

Hindsight is 20/20

As with most AI uses, Posh Technologies is building a data-hungry platform that requires massive amounts of information for it to succeed. Cutting themselves off from valuable information sources so early on may have delayed their success.

There were a few things that Posh acknowledges they should have pursued earlier: more ambitious research experiments, early focus on a domain, and keeping up with open source advances. Despite Posh's academic pedigree—they started as researchers in MIT's AI Language Lab—they didn't initially realize the importance of pursuing bold internal research experiments and the impact that would have on their AI success.

The fear of competition kept them insulated from some of their peers, too. They missed valuable early networking opportunities with other experts in their field. By staying siloed early on, they could have secured a deeper understanding of the broad industry. After working with others, they've seen the value in sharing knowledge and tapping into the broader open source community. Today, Posh celebrates the open source movement for a freer, more democratic approach to innovation. Furthermore, with a more collaborative strategy—especially with industry partners, customers, and peers—Posh builds community and increase their credibility.

Next Steps for Posh Technologies

Posh has used mostly supervised machine learning to get where they are. Although supervised machine learning is an incredibly powerful tool, it requires significant human input. And it doesn't just call for mountains of data—it needs annotated data, which is notoriously hard to come by.

Recently, Posh has been moving toward a hybrid approach, where unsupervised machine learning presents a huge opportunity. Unsupervised learning would allow their computers to develop their own rules and understandings of trends, patterns, and categories. More importantly, it would eliminate Posh's reliance on annotated data.

They're in the market now, but they're still improving (as is the case with all AI). As language algorithms get more advanced, there's only one pressing issue left:

Finding chatbots with better knock-knock jokes.

Why NLP Is So Popular

After your hundredth spam call (or a few minutes of talking with SmarterChild), speaking with computers can get pretty old, pretty quick. Or at least, that's how it used to be. Today, conversations with computers are more intuitive, enjoyable, and productive.

One of the reasons why NLP is so popular now is because the stakes are lower than when interacting with a human. You can read a message and choose never to respond again without feeling rude.

Finn AI is well aware of this, and they've used it to their advantage. By using NLP, they make it easy financial institutions to engage with humans who avoid other humans. It all comes down to customer acquisition and care.

AI Case Study
Finn AI

> One curious trend, especially among younger generations, is an aversion to calling people. In some circles, calling someone instead of texting them is an unforgivable sin.
>
> So, why is that?
>
> Texting is a form of human interaction mediated by time and permission. Time, in that interlocutors can give themselves more time to respond, and permission, in that every read and sent message represents the active choice to read and respond. Basically, people feel more in control—

and less obligated to remain fully engaged—in text-based communication. They maintain the conversation on their own terms.

In the same vein, voice-based applications are rapidly picking up pace. The rapid adoption of voice assistants like Amazon's Alexa and Apple's Siri show that it's not the "talking" part of conversation that humans don't like—it's the other humans. Capitalizing on these trends are companies like Finn AI.

Finn AI is a banking chatbot and assistant. It helps customers perform normal online and mobile banking functions, plus it can direct queries, provide customer support, recommend products and services, and offer financial counseling and advice. Finn AI believes that online and mobile banking are evolving to be more personalized and human-like. They expect people to use more conversational interfaces and voice-activated banking in the future.

How Finn AI Works

Finn AI's stack is built on Amazon Web Services and, like Posh Technologies, it relies on Amazon

Turk for data. Because their chatbot is their main user interface, Finn AI focuses primarily on NLP. Working only in the financial sector helps simplify Finn AI's development—it doesn't have to train on other subject matter in order to be complete. Instead, it's free to specialize in banking terms and conversation.

Fortunately, there's a lot of data available in the banking world. As more people speak with chatbots, the chatbots process banking conversations with more accuracy. That cuts down on model training time. Typically, Finn AI begins delivering value within 3–6 months (depending on the use case), which is much faster than the usual development cycle for banks. Not only that, but Finn AI's technology already works out of the box—it continues to train during deployment, but there's no waiting period before it's functional.

Finn AI Primary Use Cases

So far, the two primary use cases for Finn AI are customer acquisition and customer care.

Their customer acquisition use case drives sales and reduces the cost of customer acquisition.

Finn AI gathers valuable personal and contact information to leverage for marketing and sales tasks, such as recommending products and services. It also reduces customer acquisition cost by acting as a first point of contact for prospective customers, replacing costly human labor.

Finn AI also assists with customer care. The primary method by which it helps here is through digital self-service. Customers can speak with Finn AI to help them troubleshoot account issues, find resources for their requests, or otherwise fix their own problems.

Machine-directed self-service support increases operational efficiency, reducing a financial institution's reliance on human agents. No longer will banks or credit unions need to hire staff to answer questions that are already clearly answered elsewhere on their website!

There are other use cases for Finn AI, but these two are their biggest selling points.

Not Always Smooth Sailing

Finn AI is performing very well so far. However, there are always hiccups in machine learning scenarios. And their struggles weren't unique. As with most AI, one of the primary issues involved data: not only does machine learning require a massive amount of data, but it also needs good data. You can't just throw a bunch of random, unstructured, or irrelevant information at it and expect it to use that data effectively. The truth is that machine learning takes a lot of manual input. Not only does sourcing data require manual labor, but so does the complicated data science work.

Aligning that data with business goals can present a problem, sometimes. For example, Finn AI is chiefly concerned with customer queries. Conversations need a natural flow to make sense to customers. You can't just go immediately from Point A to Point B—you have to think of the customer's conversational journey. The chatbot can't take a circuitous route either, or customers will get frustrated and lose patience. Nobody wants to go from Point A to Point D, then to Point L and Point S, back to point E, then forward to Point X, until finally Point B comes. That would be a very obnoxious, convoluted conversation, and not at all human-like.

Ensuring access to the right Application Program Interfaces (APIs) and design components is critical for fluid conversation. Without them, the conversational interface—and the natural language processing—just doesn't feel, well, natural.

Another issue that Finn AI had to work through was customer expectations. Finn AI is a chatbot that can help direct users to resources, but it's not a resource in and of itself. One such instance of this was with problem-solving opportunities: Finn AI can show people how to reset their passwords, but it doesn't have the ability to reset their password for them. In that sense, one of Finn AI's early (and ongoing) issues is in educating its users about what problems it's actually designed to solve. As Morpheus from *The Matrix* said, it "can only show you the door—you're the one who has to walk through it."

Think of it as more of a tour guide than an advanced digital personal assistant.

What's Next for Finn AI

Finn AI's current issues have less to do with technology and more to do with implementation. Each financial institution is different. Accordingly, they allocate resources in different ways, prioritize different services, and adopt technology at different speeds. Finn AI is already being used by several banks in the US, and the demand for their service is increasing rapidly.

However, being a B2B2C player complicates things. Finn AI's team is responsible for the success of their product both in the hands of the financial institution and in the hands of their customers or members. It's a challenge, but Finn AI helps banks and credit unions with placement of their chatbot. After all, getting their interface in front of the financial institution's customers is one of the final pieces of the puzzle.

Aside from that, the future is bright. Their sights are set less on development and more on refining and scaling their product. And, with the rapid adoption of similar services, as well as people's tendency to avoid speaking with other humans, Finn AI is well-placed for the future.

NLP Isn't on Its Way—It's Here

Just in case you were wondering if NLP is still a few years away from hitting prime time, I want to assure you that it's already here. It's been in the limelight for a while now. And it's well-established in our industry.

By now you've probably heard the rumors. But maybe you've been living under a rock for the last few years. Or maybe you just really hate reading about technological developments in the financial industry. (If that's the case, you've made a strange choice in picking up this book.) Either way, let me introduce Erica.

Erica from Bank of America

Erica is Bank of America's AI chatbot application. Erica is powered by two forms of AI: predictive analytics and NLP. Erica's mission is to act as a financial assistant; it helps customers access account information, transfer or send money, schedule meetings, and cover basic customer service requests.

Bank of America launched Erica to the limited market of Rhode Island in March of 2018. Within a month, it had a million users. Somebody must have forgotten that Rhode Island isn't an actual island though, and word got out. Soon after Erica's debut, other markets were clamoring for it. By April, it expanded to five more states, and by June it was everywhere.

Erica's ability to search across all accounts, including debit and credit cards, aids users with day-to-day banking. But Erica has some curious functionality as well, such as tap and gesture features. With those, users don't even have to type in the conversation—similar to navigating a phone screen, the AI interface is navigable and provides easy banking options based on gestural input. And Erica learns quickly, thanks to machine learning and NLP. One thing that surprised me was that it understands imperfect English and slang, so if you ask about "dough," it knows that you mean "cash." The AI sorts through context clues quickly and provides accurate answers.

Erica isn't exactly groundbreaking technology, either. At the time of this book's publication, it's been live for years. Still, a voice-banking chatbot that handles easy customer service requests saw usage by half of its bank's customers within six months of its public launch. That should indicate how fast consumers are willing to adopt technology now.

The pace of adoption tends to mirror the pace of progress. Lightbulbs took forever to saturate the market, and ATMs took decades. Smartphones took several years. Erica took months. People are more trusting of and ready for change today than they have ever been. And they're used to it, too. Just imagine the rate of adoption for future technologies. (The following graph may help you visualize it better.)

Tech Adoption Rates

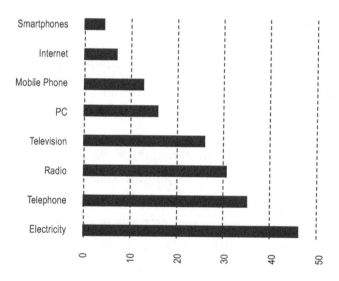

Years taken until adopted by 25% of the U.S. population

Ultimately though, there is growing consumer demand for automated self-service options. As most digital solutions show, people consistently value one thing above a friendly face: convenience. Convenience is a better indicator of consumer loyalty than general satisfaction. Furthermore, it accelerates technological adoption—probably because people will do whatever it takes to be lazier!

So, while some companies like Posh Technologies and Finn AI are creating solutions specifically for banking purposes, other companies are using richer, broader data sets in non-financial use cases to fuel their foray into the financial industry. For example, Verloop is building on its success in global real estate, telecom, ecommerce, etc. By training their AI across numerous industries—including banking, financial services, and insurance—they feel they've developed a well-rounded product.

It certainly raises the question: would you prefer a chatbot trained only for financial institutions? Or would you be more comfortable with a chatbot that can leverage data from other markets?

Don't worry—there is no right answer.

The Big Takeaway

There are many use cases of AI in financial services today. It's easy to see where institutions could get started. And there's no reason to fear adoption. At this point, people expect innovation. They eagerly await the latest developments and conveniences. And if they don't get the latest? Well, they just might find a competitor who can give them what they want.

Fortunately, AI can help them find just the right one.

8

ACCOUNT RETENTION

Financial institutions spend an average minimum of $350–400 to acquire each account holder. But that's just the first step. It costs even more money to market various products and services to existing members or customers. It would be a shame to lose those accounts after such substantial investments.

So, how do you ensure that the people who've chosen your financial institution stay with you? How do you make sure the loan you've given them doesn't move to another organization? If you've issued someone a credit card, how do you make certain that they'll continue to use it?

These are addressable problems, but they haven't yet been solved. ANI offers better results and measurable improvements when it comes to keeping the business that you worked for. Two new fintechs come to mind when I think about keeping customers and increasing loyalty. Those two fintechs are Digital Onboarding and WalletFi.

AI Case Study
Digital Onboarding

25–40% of those new accounts leave their financial institution within a year. As tempting as it is to assign blame, it might not be the best use of anyone's time. The statistic speaks for itself: new account holders don't always fully commit to their financial institution right off the bat.

The credit union-specific Digital Onboarding platform from Digital Onboarding, Inc. increases member retention by maximizing engagement in the days (and months) following the opening of a first account. The platform triggers email and SMS reminders that link to personalized, step-by-step digital guides that introduce new members to relevant products and account-related services.

After investing to bring in new accounts, credit unions stand to lose a lot of money from churn. Members who leave quickly—or worse, open a checking account and never use it—hurt the credit union's income statement. Engaging members from the start results in longer, more profitable, and more satisfying relationships.

How the Digital Onboarding Platform Works

The Digital Onboarding platform motivates new credit union members to learn about and enroll in account-related services such as online and mobile banking, direct deposits, and bill pay. It also encourages adoption of other relevant products such as credit cards, auto loans, CDs, and high-yield savings accounts.

In the financial world, people who open only checking accounts tend to have higher attrition rates than people who open both checking and savings accounts. The more accounts, products, and services they use, the less likely they are to leave. People who join institutions for low auto loan rates don't often investigate the other available benefits or opportunities. By creating greater engagement with the credit union, the Digital Onboarding platform increases the likelihood that new members will be satisfied and stick around for the long haul.

Like every company in this book, Digital Onboarding, Inc. will use AI to accomplish its goals. They company plans to use machine learning two ways: tactically and strategically (for targeting).

For strategic targeting, Digital Onboarding, Inc. encourages credit unions to use its platform to automatically identify the best members for a particular product, service, or other offer.

The platform's machine learning capability will help credit unions automatically identify:

> Which members qualify for specific products and account-related services

> Which members are most likely to need particular products or services

Which accounts are at risk of closing (so the credit union can re-engage them before it's too late)

The platform's automated, AI-based targeting personalizes marketing messaging. It also helps new and less-engaged members explore relevant products and services at their credit union.

Tactically, the Digital Onboarding platform automatically identifies and suggests optimal outreach strategies. It finds the best days and hours to send SMS and email reminders. Typically, those tactical decisions are made by people. Their decisions are supposedly based on reason, but usually they're arbitrary. Machine learning analyzes data more quickly and accurately than humans, which allows it to quickly identify the best times and methods of outreach, which leads to higher engagement, cross selling opportunities, and service enrollment.

Using a neural network requires a massive amount of data to effectively do anything. So, where does Digital Onboarding, Inc. get that data?

Digital Onboarding, Inc. developed an efficient, collaborative solution: because most credit unions don't have the volume of data needed to make accurate predictions, the platform shares insights across financial institutions without compromising confidentiality. Thus, the Digital Onboarding platform can leverage data from Credit Union A for Community Bank B, and vice versa, since most institutions have the same objectives (cross selling a particular product or motivating a member to enroll in a service like direct deposit or digital banking. The result is a richer pool of insights from which to draw, which maximizes performance.

Part of what makes Digital Onboarding, Inc. so effective is its mission. Rather than asking new members to figure things out themselves, they guide them toward their best options. Onboarding and account management become friendlier, more manageable tasks. The platform nudges people to take better control over their finances. And Digital Onboarding, Inc. isn't the only company trying to make sure that your business stays your business. Another fintech, WalletFi, focuses less on customer acquisition and more on keeping your card top of wallet. WalletFi leverages ANI to keep card users informed and empowered so they can make the best spending decisions available.

Not only that, but they reduce the friction and churn that comes with card-related issues that lead to card replacement.

AI Case Study
WalletFi

Imagine this: you recently took a little vacation. However, while on your trip, your card was lost or stolen. You have to cancel your card to keep unscrupulous vagabonds from racking up an unbelievable bar tab or buying a lifetime supply of Doritos. (Both highly likely scenarios, I'm sure.)

Unfortunately, that means you now have to set up new recurring payment plans with your replacement card. Fortunately, WalletFi helps consumers manage their recurring subscriptions and payments. They facilitate seamless transitions from one card to the next on a single, centralized platform. Plus, they keep people aware of their monthly expenditures, which leads to smarter, healthier budgeting.

WalletFi for Smarter Card Management

Here are some easy statistics to remember:

- As of 2019, the average American consumer has 2.35 credit cards, and most people have at least one debit card.

- By the beginning of 2018, about 50% of American adults signed up for at least one subscription service*.

- WalletFi's studies indicate that the average American spends between $850 and $1,000 per month on recurring payments and subscriptions.

When you add it all up, that comes to a lot of different monthly payments across several different payment methods. Not only that, but transitions from old cards to new causes account churn and

....

* These subscriptions include things like Amazon Prime, Netflix, Dollar Shave Club, Blue Apron, and Birch Box. Other recurring payments include more mundane necessities such as car insurance, utility bills, mobile phone plans, gym memberships, and health insurance.

pain for the financial institution. Often, this churn loses the financial institution's place as the user's top of wallet.

But it doesn't have to. WalletFi offers consumers the ability to switch their subscriptions and recurring payments from one card to the next. If a card is lost or stolen, users can update their new card's information in the app, then switch all their recurring payments from their old card to their new one.

This also provides a major opportunity for the issuing institution. They can incentivize the use of their own card through the app. In so doing, not only do they provide transparency, control, and convenience—they also provide a reason to move their card to the consumer's top of wallet. Considering the average American expenditure on recurring payments, that comes to quite a big chunk of interchange revenue.

How WalletFi Does It

WalletFi leverages machine learning to recognize recurring payments. Their platform can differentiate between recurring and non-recurring charges over any time period, whether it be weekly, monthly, annually, or any other interval.

WalletFi's machine learning taxonomizes recurring transactions after reviewing several dozen separate data points. Yet, despite the computing power and speed of machine learning, WalletFi's algorithms perform best after about 13 months of historical data, allowing time for spending patterns to be established and annual subscriptions (like Amazon Prime) to be identified.

It's not that WalletFi doesn't work immediately—it does. It's highly functional from the start, but it also refines itself per individual user. Over time, a user's algorithm becomes unique to them, and it's better able to categorize their transactions and provide tangible, actionable insights.

Before WalletFi used machine learning to taxonomize transaction types, it used more traditional methods. First, they created a whitelist of merchants. The list included notable subscriptions such as Spotify, Hulu, and HelloFresh. WalletFi then matched their results against transaction reports from Plaid and Yodlee to confirm accuracy. However, the algorithm identified only whitelisted merchants, which were mostly large, and nationally popular. It missed a lot of local vendors like utility companies, insurance companies, gym memberships, and so on.

So, what did they do?

They changed from a whitelist model to a basic algorithm that looked for monthly charges. It was an improvement, but it still had problems. One issue that kept cropping up was the "Chipotle" problem that FlexPay ran into. Some of WalletFi's beta testers confused the algorithm by eating too often at particular restaurants—popular places like Subway, Chipotle, and Five Guys were being miscategorized as recurring charges.

Obviously, that didn't work for WalletFi or its testers. To more effectively differentiate between frequent charges and actual subscriptions, they turned to machine learning. It took WalletFi about two years to start seeing the results they wanted to see. After their first year, they realized they needed more data. A lot more data.

They looked for thousands of transaction records to train their algorithm. Machine learning requires a colossal amount of information. They worked with 500 beta testers to test and refine their system. However, that proved insufficient, and neither public nor for-profit datasets of day-to-day transaction data were useful. To find their own data, they created WalletFi Lite—a no-integration-required product that allowed financial institutions to send their transaction datasets for analysis. With WalletFi Lite, they've processed around 10 million transactions, leading to a much-improved identification algorithm.

Their goal is to correctly classify 90% of all transactions. And while it might be technically possible to develop a classification model that doesn't use machine learning, it could take countless hundreds of hours to develop, test, and revise. Machine learning is there to cut that development time down to a fraction of that time.

What's Next for WalletFi

WalletFi is partnering with financial institutions to increase retention and facilitate personalized member experiences during acquisitions, mergers, and card (re)issuance events. WalletFi will help institutions better understand and target consumers for incentives and rewards based on their different subscriptions. This will deepend relationships with account holders and increase institutional share of wallet and interchange. (After all, just as Gretzky misses 100% of shots he doesn't take, financial institutions also lose 100% of the interchange of the transactions that aren't on their card.)

In that vein, the card update process can be a pain. WalletFi hopes that providing consumers a pain-free way to manage and switch recurring payments between cards will show the value that financial institutions offer in reducing friction and frustration.

WalletFi also wants to continue helping consumers make better financial decisions. One of the benefits they saw early on was in identifying areas where people can save money or spend smarter. For example, let's say three members of a family are all paying for Spotify subscriptions. WalletFi can highlight their overlapping subscriptions and potentially save them money by letting them know there's a family plan available.

Essentially, WalletFi's primary objective is to make life easier when it's time to update and manage payment methods for recurring charges and subscriptions. Machine learning has been key to unlocking that potential.

So now, imagine this: you just got back from vacation where your card went MIA. After you canceled it and received a new one, you logged into your WalletFi app, pressed a couple buttons and *voila*! Everything's set.

It's clearly a great service, and it's one that is validated by Wells Fargo's release of their *Control Tower* in their digital banking app. So, obviously it has broad appeal. And letting customers and members know about the service could be really easy, too. An NLP chatbot could introduce it. After all, you do remember Digital Onboarding, right?

The Big Takeaway

Two different AI products that work toward the same goal can coexist. One could argue that rather than competing with each other (or just limiting the other's efficacy), two different AI solutions can strengthen each other, making each better than they normally would be. Thus, tying a couple services together could build an incredibly dynamic digital ecosystem. Your institution can facilitate rapid adoption of new technologies, services, and account types among its customers.

With WalletFi and Digital Onboarding, the idea is to ensure your financial institution doesn't lose business to its competitors or their products. But what happens if you aren't all that worried about competitors? What if your whole goal is to help your already loyal customers find what they need? In that case, you'd need something to handle lending and product recommendations.

9

LENDING AND PRODUCT RECOMMENDATIONS

For some reason, people like *money* and *stuff*. Accordingly, people search them out constantly. Just think of how successful your financial institution could be if it offered *money* and *stuff*—or the equivalents. And, if you made interest, fees, or interchange from offering them, you could significantly increase your margin.

One way to offer people *stuff* is through next best product recommendations. For financial institutions, the products are rarely (if ever) big fancy things like cars and boats and giant stuffed unicorns. Often, they're CDs, premium cards, and the like. Still, those are the kind of products that can generate both short- and long-term financial viability for consumers.

ANI algorithms are preternaturally adept at figuring out what *stuff* people want, and then finding the product that can help them get it. With big *stuff* like cars, boats, and houses, next best product models show available loan terms and financing options.

That's where *money* comes in. Financial institutions can't exactly go around handing out money just because people want it. However, they can hand out money when people agree to pay it back (and can prove they're good for it). Still, it can cost a lot to assess creditworthiness and underwrite loans. Fortunately, ANI algorithms can streamline that process as well. And they can do it with or without traditional credit models like FICO.

The best part? They can do it more accurately, too. I'd like to present a few AI banking products that give people money.

AI Case Study
Loanify, Inc.

First, let's talk about *stuff*, the first half of the *money + stuff* equation. Financial institutions don't sell turntables, vacuum cleaners, and other Amazon items. But they will help people buy cars.

The market for used vehicles is huge. It's around twice the size of the new car industry, and it's growing. Furthermore, it's less susceptible to market fluctuations and recessions. So, financial institutions that can provide seamless, end-to-end used car shopping experiences are best positioned to help their account holders find their next car—and capture the attendant loan revenue.

That's precisely what Loanify does. They partner with credit unions to educate members about the car-buying process and offer simple purchase options. And it all starts with an app.

Understanding Loanify

Of car shoppers who get pre-approved for an auto loan at a credit union, only around half of them actually use that loan to buy a car. Those who don't use the credit union's loan often turn to dealer financing. Loanify, through their Fast-Pass Mobile app, guides members through the car buying process, ensuring they get the best financing option available.

Loanify's app activates when shoppers enter the premises of any franchise auto dealership. Immediately as they arrive, it offers proof of their pre-approved auto loan. This is critical to show dealerships that the buyer is serious and that they understand their budget.

Additionally, the app provides access to educational materials about auto purchasing, thus guaranteeing people make informed, advantageous buying decisions. Plus, besides general buying education and information, the FastPass Mobile app offers major support in the form of AI and human assistance. That is, potential buyers can use the AI to check the value of their trade in, see typical prices or terms, and otherwise explore the world of car financing. Or, if the buyer wants to speak to a credit union representative, they can simply chat with an available expert.

Simultaneously, the FastPass app alerts the credit union that a member has entered a car dealership. The Loanify AI can determine the likelihood of purchase, so that committed buyers can get extra care while they're on the lot.

Loanify puts the credit union in the buyer's corner after they walk into a dealership. Buyers are protected form dealers who would talk them out of their best financing options, and credit unions stay in the running for financing options.

How Loanify Works

Loanify and its FastPass Mobile app strengthen the relationship between members and their credit unions during the car buying process. But how does it work?

As you may have guessed, they use two different forms of AI. The first form is machine learning, which gives buyers accurate, up-to-date numbers for prices, trade-in values, gap insurance, mechanical coverage, and more. This AI is far more trustworthy than the dealership, and it's faster and more reliable than cruising through various sites like *Edmunds* and *Kelley Blue Book*. It uses the next best product engine to suggest appropriate terms for any transaction.

But their AI doesn't stop there. Loanify also powers their app with NLP. This NLP allows members to chat and interact with their app intuitively, asking questions and receiving answers in an accessible, understandable way. Potential buyers can thus get insight about pricing, gap insurance, and so on.

Both types of AI work in tandem to assess the buyer's situation and offer insight quickly, easily, and without complication.

What's Next for Loanify

As with almost every case study in this book, Loanify wouldn't have minded more data to work with. Even though financial data is structured and relatively easy for AI to understand, the quantity is just as important as the quality.

As Loanify grows and partners with more credit unions, they'll gain more transactional data to leverage for even more accurate predictions and recommendations.

At this point, most of their energy is focused on business growth rather than AI growth. Their AI models perform very well—a product of a great development team. However, despite having a strong product, they feel the biggest area of growth ahead is in hitting the market.

Every company that works with AI knows that improving algorithms and sourcing data is an ongoing task. Loanify is no exception. But for now, their focus is on getting that technology in the hands of the people who need it.

Loanify, Inc. helps people buy cars while ensuring that dealerships don't cut lenders out of the financing picture. It's just one way that financial institutions can help people get *stuff*. But some people need *money* more, and especially in times of emergencies or other significant setbacks. Getting a small loan quickly—as in, fully funded in less than a minute—is often the difference between useful money and a missed opportunity (or worse). QCash's AI can handle that .

AI Case Study
QCash

Purveyors of short-term credit and small-dollar loans have gotten an understandably bad rap in the last couple decades. And it makes sense—before regulations, some interest rates on these loans went as high as 1,000%. Even today, short-term loan interest rates climb over 600% in some states. In many ways, the reputation that short-term credit earned was, well, *earned*. But it doesn't have to be that way. And frankly, it shouldn't be.

The fact is that in 2020, the apparent health of the economy and the unemployment rate belie the financial reality for most Americans. Nearly 80% of American workers live paycheck to paycheck. Almost 40% of Americans wouldn't afford a $400 emergency expense. While the economy is certainly benefiting some, those benefits aren't necessarily trickling down to everyone.

QCash entered the short-term lending marketplace to deliver necessary services to credit union members. They used (and recommend) interest rates only slightly higher than normal personal loan interest rates, which kept things fair for borrowers and worthwhile for their credit union.

Understanding QCash

QCash was founded in 2003, when the Washington State Employee's Credit Union CEO noticed that their members were paying millions of dollars in fees per year at nearby payday loan centers. That presented a few problems:

> The high interest rates at payday loan centers were jeopardizing borrowers' long-term financial viability.

> Credit unions were failing to provide members with critical small loan services.

> Credit unions were missing out on potential loan interest revenue.

To provide a safer alternative, they developed a system for underwriting and funding quick loans.

Their system relied on traditional measures of creditworthiness, such as FICO scores. It proved clunky and unprofitable for years. Loans took too long to underwrite and fund, and the whole program was costing them money. Using FICO scores, many creditworthy people didn't get approved for loans for which they should have qualified. Other times, people with no business borrowing got approved for loans they struggled to repay.

QCash knew they had to do away with that. They were missing too many opportunities to help their members. In 2015, QCash realized that they had the data to expand their loan offerings even further. Analytics powered by machine learning allowed QCash to look beyond FICO scores for determining creditworthiness. Instead, they used broader data, including less-tangible statistics based on the relationship between the member and the credit union. Now, a member's history with the credit union, their account types, and their banking habits all contribute to QCash's automated underwriting algorithm.

Those underwriting models are fast, too. They're faster than traditional methods of measuring a borrower's creditworthiness, largely because they don't need to pull any reports. The speed that they underwrite--and fund—loans is particularly useful for members who can't wait for their cash. From application to full funding, QCash can deliver loans in 60 seconds.

When you consider how high-risk short-term credit is, their loan loss rate is particularly impressive. They stay in the single digits, with an average loss of 6–8%. They manage all this without resorting to predatory lending techniques or outrageously high interest rates.

How QCash Works

Okay, so QCash can underwrite and fund a profitable loan quickly by leveraging aspects of AI. But how did they do it?

Today, QCash uses Microsoft machine learning platform, Azure. QCash eventually settled on a model that was easy to explain to regulators—uncomplicated inputs and outputs kept them out of unnecessary trouble.

In fact, demonstrating algorithms, equations, inputs, and outputs has been an issue for regulators in the past. Yet, as machine learning increases in popularity and efficacy, people who work with the technology are getting better about showing their work rather than showing only their answers. So long as knowledge about and usage of machine learning increases, companies that rely on aspects of AI can rest assured that presenting, explaining, and defending their technology will get easier.

Fortunately for QCash, their simple machine learning model has been extremely effective so far. After a few years of trial, error, and feature engineering, their machine learning dropped delinquent payments from 7% to just over 5% over a 65-day period. That's an impressive 20% improvement over baseline.

How QCash Could Have Improved Their Process

QCash's employees all started as expert IT and finance staff. They were in business, but they were not businesspeople. They knew how to build their product, but they struggled to sell it. Thus, the road to adoption was very slow—typical of community financial institutions. Still, running a data-driven enterprise means that they have numbers to back up their claims. As they collected data, they proved that their service works.

On the technical side of things, QCash wishes they knew which direction the machine learning landscape was headed. As early adopters of the technology, they tried several platforms before finding a setup that they like. For example, although they currently use Python and Microsoft Azure, they didn't start there. The whole landscape was much less standardized then than it is now. But as AI technologies become more commonplace, some platforms are clear frontrunners, and wading into AI projects is less of a crapshoot.

As it stands, though, there's one bit of the early process that they don't regret: timing. They could have waited a couple years to get started, but they didn't wait until the technology was further ahead. Why? Because they knew how important data is to machine learning. They bought into the need for data early, and it's paid off: they can show proof of their model predicting with more accuracy than the credit bureau.

What's Next for QCash

One of QCash's next moves to increase their explainability for underwriting, particularly with more advanced machine learning models.

As QCash grows, they're also investigating ways to improve collections. On their short-term road map, they're working on a collections model for non-real-estate loans. Their hope is that they'll be able to apply a better collections model for their expanding loan portfolio.

Finally, QCash aims to expand their use of analytics. They believe that more data will improve their accuracy. This goal—and this understanding of the primacy of data—aligns with the goals of every AI industry player. Plus, analytics will reinforce their underwriting capabilities.

One thing that QCash wants financial institutions to know is that machine learning isn't scary. It still has a way to go as far as simplicity and accessibility, but that's changing quickly. As far as the near future is concerned, they expect machine learning to take a more prominent role in the financial sector.

The Big Takeaway

QCash and Loanify are just two of many companies entering the AI lending marketplace. There are many opportunities for growth here, from upselling and cross-selling, to financial stability, to the financial empowerment of those who need it most. If you are looking for a way to both increase your margin and to provide a safety net to your most vulnerable members and customers, then this is one area to give a closer look.

It isn't only the smaller players who are experimenting with what AI can bring to the table—it's the large ones, too. And the large ones have the resources to make big moves. If you can't provide your members or customers with fast credit or short-term loans, what happens when a major bank debuts the same service? Or if they develop more accurate methods for determining creditworthiness before you, increasing their profitability and competitiveness?

AI is already entering the mainstream. That's why I'm writing this book with such a sense of urgency. People want *money* and *stuff*, and they'll find the institutions best able to provide them.

10

IMPROVED
SERVICE

All the technology in the world isn't worth a darn if people hate your financial institution. One of the most important—and more frequently overlooked—parts of success is the people who helped you achieve it. I'm not talking about business partners here. No, this is about the lifeblood of your financial institution: your members and customers. Fortunately, there are several ways to improve the services you offer your members and customers.

Service is a very broad category, and it was hard to choose just a couple examples of how AI can (or does) improve it. Nevertheless, I'll try to pick two.

First, there's Narmi. In Narmi's case, they provide people with intuitive, personalized online and mobile banking experiences. They prize transparent and relevant banking, modernized financial services, and integrations with popular apps through their online and mobile banking platform. This sets each user up with an individualized, empowering portal to their financial life.

On the other end of the spectrum, we have Envel. Envel gives people an individualized banking experience too, except their approach is tough love. They develop tailored banking plans for each user designed to enforce healthy, sustainable financial habits.

Both fintechs think of the user first. They may be banking providers at heart, but their primary focus is on fulfilling a need for their users. It's critical that financial institutions moving toward AI remember that they shouldn't think only of themselves—everyone can benefit from technological progress. Now, let me show you what they're made of.

AI Case Study
Narmi

Large banks have seemingly endless resources to develop and maintain strong digital banking support. Many people—especially those in younger generations—expect seamless, digital-first approaches to banking. However, most financial institutions are regional or community banks and credit unions. For them, developing seamless, digital-first banking platforms is very difficult.

Although some smaller financial institutions have made commendable progress toward establishing vibrant digital options, most are falling sorely behind. It's tough keeping up with the Joneses when the Joneses have things like:

> Intuitive online banking
>
> Comprehensive mobile banking
>
> Fast and hassle-free digital onboarding
>
> Engaging and navigable web design
>
> Industry-leading saving, budgeting, and financial wellness features
>
> An open banking API
>
> High-quality technical support

Pursuing such broad, critical capabilities in this digital age requires a massive amount of time, energy, and money. For many financial institutions, the cost of implementing cutting-edge, digital-forward solutions and online banking services is untenable. And yet, that's what Narmi offers smaller institutions: the digital banking capabilities of large banks and fintechs.

How Narmi Does It

The name of the game is personalization. Most people don't want a one-size-fits-all solution thrown at them—they want to be understood. Credit unions and banks must cater to individuals to provide the kind of experiences they expect: convenient ones.

Researchers at Harvard found that customer loyalty is determined largely by the effort it takes to accomplish something. People prefer brands, products, and services that require minimal effort. Whichever option asks people to jump through the fewest hoops, wins.

Narmi works to understand member and customer needs. Their platform is designed to get people what they want as quickly and painlessly as possible. Increasing convenience for users means doing a lot more work behind the scenes to differentiate users, preferences, and spending habits. They accurately predict what a person wants and needs according to their financial data. Most importantly, they work fast and their platform is scalable. The only way to do all that is with AI.

Currently, Narmi employs several machine learning techniques. They use in-house models to make things more legible to humans. Narmi also uses Amazon's machine learning platform for convenience and security applications. For example, Amazon helps them with voice banking, blocking DDoS attacks, and identity verification.

> Distributed Denial of Service (DDoS) attacks are when multiple computers or systems act in concert to overwhelm a server with internet traffic. If you can imagine what happens when a five-lane highway narrows to a single lane during rush hour, then you can imagine what happens to a server's ability to handle congested internet traffic. Basically, a crash is going to occur.
>
> RE: DDoS

What's Next for Narmi?

Foremost among Narmi's concerns is providing immediate value to their financial institutions. They're working with the kind of tools they need to improve revenue generation for their clients. For example, their machine learning can help financial institutions automatically identify their most valuable customers to send targeted, customized offers, and tailor marketing efforts to individual account holders. This kind of sales and lead generation support improves customer and member engagement, leading to long-term, profitable relationships. That kind of individualized approach benefits the financial institution's members as well. They'll be better informed about relevant products and services, which could introduce them to higher-yield accounts, better savings strategies, and investment opportunities.

Another use for machine learning on Narmi's horizon will help with risk management and compliance. AI will soon be able to help with loss prevention, including issues such as fraud detection, account takeovers, and more. Narmi expects AI and machine learning to be of critical importance when it comes to asset optimization and other liabilities related to compression.

Narmi is already well established in the market. Not only do they work with many banks and credit unions, but they've also partnered with other fintechs and financial service providers to broaden their functionality. Their aggressive pursuit of convenience for their users—as well as the value they offer their financial institutions—is impressive, and there's no doubt that they will continue to push into the world of AI to expand and optimize their capabilities in the future.

Not all heroes wear capes, though. While Narmi wants to offer users all the options in the world—or at least all the options that each user might possibly want—Envel wants to caution against that freedom. Founder Dimitri Artamonov claims that the dream scenario with Envel is for a user to be in a shoe store with a $500 pair of boots that they can't realistically afford, and then getting their card declined and feeling embarrassed in front of the entire line. "That's the kind of emotional support people need," he says.

So, how would that work?

AI Case Study
Envel

Although it comes easy to some, most people aren't great at budgeting. Unfortunately, the cost of budgeting poorly can be high. If you overdraft your account, you get a fine. That fine impacts your budget further, and it also hurts your credit. Poor budgeting can lead to a downward spiral of charges, fees, and credit card or loan debt.

But what if your financial institution helped you budget? What if it could enforce that budget? What if let you know how much money you had to spend each month? Each week? Each day, even? Then, if you reached your budget for the day, the institution could cut off access to non-essential spending. You wouldn't overdraft your account. You wouldn't get fines. If you got cut off when you tried to buy a case of beer or new sunglasses, your budget would be fine, and the only thing to suffer would be your pride.

That's what Envel wants to offer its users: the ability to regain control of their finances through an AI-determined budget.

Their end goals?

> To provide better value through banking

> To automate financial management by creating budgets and managing money

> To help underprivileged and young people save for the future and better control their finances—especially if they never had the opportunity or the means to develop healthy financial habits

They're noble goals, and they're not easy to attain, but someone's gotta do it. That someone just might be Envel.

How They're Doing It

Envel's platform draws from several areas of AI. Each type of AI technology they use plays a slightly different, complementary role in their service.

Amazon's machine learning handles prediction and budgeting with both supervised and unsupervised machine learning models. Envel also uses machine learning for grouping and clustering purposes. This helps them categorize user segments and understand myriad complex financial situations. NLP is in the mix too, where Envel hopes that chatbots can help them with sales and customer service.

If their comfort with several different types of AI is any indication, Envel doesn't mind trying several solutions to see which one works best. Before using Amazon, Envel was working with Microsoft's AI, Azure. In many ways, Azure was a more intuitive, pliable platform—however, Envel felt that their algorithms weren't as efficient as they should be. Following Microsoft's Azure, Envel moved to using an open source stack. They loved the customization it allowed, but they needed more stability. Finally, Amazon made them an offer that they couldn't refuse.

One of the curious aspects of Envel is that they're far more than a run-of-the-mill technological financial service. In attempting to understand various spending habits, they found that they were dipping into the territory of the humanities and social sciences. Envel was dealing with human behaviors. They needed accurate data about how people earned, saved, and spent, by they also needed to know why.

But accuracy is key to getting useful results from machine learning. Their algorithms wouldn't work with false answers. And people often lie to other people (such as financial planners) for fear of judgment. So, Envel wasn't sure if people would be more honest with computers—or if they'd find it even easier to lie. A few of the questions they had to ask themselves included:

Can personal financial trainers be replaced by machine learning?

Is human interaction a necessary part of financial planning?

Does strategic human interaction complement digital interfaces or NLP interactions?

Are people more or less honest with machines than they are with humans?

Ultimately, Envel decided that machine learning added significant value over traditional human interactions. Although machines aren't very empathetic, they're also not very judgmental. Envel figured that the lack of personal contact was a strength in budgeting, rather than a weakness.

Envel's Biggest Hurdle Was Conceptual

Envel set out to help younger, lower-income people take control of their finances through smarter spending and safer saving. Unfortunately, they misunderstood who needed help, and why they needed it.

Envel brought with them many several preconceived notions about how people manage their money. Many of those notions may have been geographic—college students in Boston were their primary targets. But the cost and standard of living in Boston are high, and so weren't representative of "average" consumer experiences.

The first thing Envel learned was that there were huge variations in how people handle their finances. There were, in fact, too many different elements in financial mismanagement among their target crowd. It's not like all of them simply threw caution to the wind and bought whatever looked shiniest at the time. In the same vein, they also weren't all spending their money on alcohol and entertainment. There were just too many contributing factors to bad budgeting.

Second, they wanted to help people develop better habits by making banking a positive experience. They wanted people to feel supported and validated in their good decisions. But financial planning can be stressful, and people build negative associations with it. Envel quickly learned that many people resist change. Telling someone that they're bad with money tends to elicit strong reactions. Think: disbelief, frustration, disagreement, and so on. Any approach that judged, chastised, or otherwise painted a user in a negative light didn't go over well. Envel realized they would have to take a more empathetic, less accusatory approach.

Finally, Envel fell into the classic fogey trap: they assumed that younger generations would be their main users because it's a highly technological way to learn to budget. However, they were surprised by which demographics expressed interest: all of them. As it turns out, practice doesn't make perfect if you're never taught how to practice!

At the time of writing, Envel is still in beta. However, their testers see Envel's effect. In preliminary testing, they've noticed that receptive users drastically improve their daily cash balance.

Envel estimates that they can help roughly 90% of their users, but they know it's a two-way street—if a person is unwilling to change their spending habits, then Envel won't be of any use. For example, cutting off a single credit card can make a big difference in daily spending, but for many people, that's easier said than done.

Today, Envel is well-versed in the machine learning and AI world. They use Python and Python tools to work with Microsoft Azure and Visual Studio, Amazon's Machine Learning and Redshift, and Reactive Native for mobile applications. All that is to say, they've got a good hang of things. It wasn't always that way, though. There are two things that Envel wishes it had known earlier:

First, they would have done—and read—more research. It's not that academic research always yields better answers, but it usually helps people ask better questions. Envel feels they may have zeroed in on what people wanted more quickly.

Second, they would have scoped out more data brokers. They knew machine learning requires a lot of data, but they would have wanted to build relationships with data brokers sooner.

What's Next for Envel

Envel has already changed part of their approach to helping people take control of their finances. There are undoubtedly more changes to come.

Their first step is to enrich some of their data. Machine learning requires a lot of it, and the richer they can get it, the better their results will be. They also want to learn more about the different facets of their clients. By learning more about how people use—or prefer to use—their money, they'll be better able to make valuable impacts on their customers' financial habits. They also intend to bring NLP and chatbots to both their own services and to their associated social media accounts. The goal is to bring a more accessible, human interface to what they do.

They also want to make personal finance a welcoming space by helping young people better understand and take control of their finances.

Financial institutions interested in Envel can take heart—Envel's technology functions as a stand-alone service. Envel's goal is to bring smarter monetary habits to everyone.

The Big Takeaway

Clearly, both Narmi and Envel took a different approach to service, but both absolutely fill a consumer need. Using ANI for service-oriented purposes could be a way to get a major leg up on the competition. Financial institutions that offer relevant, customized support to their members and customers have a major competitive advantage over those who merely offer the same old one-size-fits-all solutions.

As with most of the companies I've highlighted, both are looking to partner with financial institutions rather than compete with them. They know their services provide value, and they know that most community-based institutions don't have the resources to put together similar products. So, banks and credit unions can reap the benefits of AI without devoting years to development.

At some point, the limiting factor in AI-improved service will be creativity, not technology. What would you like to provide if you had the technology? As more things become possible with AI, your ideas could become realities. However, if you wait too long to get started down that road, then someone else may realize their dreams first, leaving you in the dust.

SECTION 3

THE AI PLAYBOOK

11

HOW YOUR FINANCIAL INSTITUTION CAN APPROACH AI

There's not exactly a "right way" to approach AI at this stage. There are several options for how to move forward, any of which might or might not work for your financial institution. The best way to know if an AI strategy will work for you is to weigh your options and decide what would work best.

One thing to think about is how you perceive your organization. Are you undergoing or prepared for digital transformation? Some of the benefits of digital transformation include faster, more efficient operations with fewer errors. But has your institution determined what digital transformation means to you, or which area(s) of it you wish to pursue?

RE: Digital Transformation

There are many definitions of digital transformation, but the main gist is that it's the process of adopting and using digital technology. It may involve converting older, manual systems to newer, computerized ones, or otherwise augmenting, replacing, redefining, or updating traditional infrastructure and approaches.

Digital transformation looks different for every business. For some, it might mean migrating legacy systems to the cloud. For another, it might mean full enterprise automation. For a third, it could mean developing a groundbreaking AI solution—or partnering with someone who can deliver that solution for less than the development would cost.

There's one key thing that's necessary for digital transformation to be effective: culture. Any organization undergoing digital transformation needs to own it, believe in it, and work toward it as a company-wide goal. It's not just for the IT department. Everyone is affected, from the C-level staffers and the board, to the entry-level employees, all the way to the consumers and end-users. It requires buy-in.

AI is basically the next step in digital transformation. Just as with digital transformation, financial institutions that want to begin working with (and seeing the benefits of) AI can't just make halfhearted attempts. They have to change the way they see themselves and their culture. They have to become AI-first.

What does it mean to be AI-first?

The rate of adoption for new technologies has been increasing alongside the rate of innovation. It took about 15 years for financial institutions to adopt online banking and bill pay. It took about 10 for mobile banking capabilities to become standard. Now, the analytics revolution is poised to take only six or seven years before widespread adoption. The first phase of AI will occur in less than five, and we're seeing the early stages of adoption in our industry already. That means that we've got a very small window of time to get on board before big banks and competing fintechs offer AI-improved services that we can't match up to.

To be AI-first means looking for ways to partner up with technology providers, develop internally, and implement AI wherever and whenever possible. It means being unafraid of the ramifications, choosing instead to recognize and embrace the changes and possibilities it will bring. Yes, there will be initial chaos, but through it all will emerge a new normal. It also means you must put systems and people in place to handle the coming changes.

In an AI-first world, there will be new ethics and compliance concerns. There will be new impacts on members, tellers, and member service representatives. My suggestion is to start with a future state and work backwards. At this stage, there are far more questions about AI than there are answers. **In fact, here are just a few of the hundreds of questions that might come up when becoming AI-first.**

Is it plausible that AI will replace 90% of the functions in the credit union today?

Is it possible that it could happen in the next decade or two?

And if yes, what would the future look like if you no longer needed to do the transaction work?

What would it look like if everyone had a unique financial product that did everything, customized to their individual needs?

What would it look like if your ALM model self-adjusted based on the financial marketplace, balance sheet, and the institution's defined risk profile?

What if computers could program themselves?

What if everything moved to natural language interactions?

The answer to these questions have huge implications for every area of banking. And with these implications come opportunities to be more relevant, more impactful, and more innovative for your members and customers. Once you feel comfortable asking these kinds of questions, then you're ready to start thinking about AI logistics. One of the first, most crucial logistical considerations is timing.

Timing of AI Outside vs. Inside the Financial Industry

You may have heard the old axiom, "timing is everything," and it has never been more applicable than in the case of AI. If you've thought about what AI can do for your institution, then you've probably already made the decision: at this point, it's less a matter of *if*, and more a matter of *when*. So, when do you start? Even as I write this in 2019, I know of only a few financial institutions that are working with in-house artificial intelligence. As you might imagine, they happen to be the largest institutions.

I know of many more that have signed on with companies like Alpha Rank, whose AI technology allows banks and credit unions to identify influencers—people whose opinions influence others—who may be valuable marketing assets. To be blunt, this is a baby step in the right direction. So much more can be accomplished if we embrace more aspects of AI in the financial realm.

I don't think I can understate how important it is to start working on projects in this space. If you haven't already completed at least one project in the AI space, you're already falling behind by at least a year.

So, what's the major barrier to getting started in this industry? Is it the cost of software? Surely, amazing software like this must be expensive, right? Nope! Most AI software is free. For example, Google's Tensorflow platform is open-source and available to everyone. Microsoft also offers their toolkit for free, and several other platforms have followed suit.

Is it the hardware cost? Does AI require access to supercomputers? Again, no. In fact, just recently, Google announced full machine learning support for Raspberry Pi computers. If you're unfamiliar with Raspberry Pi (not the pastry), it's a $35 computer which, for another $100, comes with a 256-gigabyte Fast SD card. For a total investment of $135, you could be machine learning tomorrow.

So, if it's not the hardware, and it's not the software, then there's one last variable. Sadly, it's the most challenging one: people. You can find a lot of people to install Tensorflow on a Raspberry Pi, and maybe you can find some people who could train it to differentiate cats and dogs (or some other AI parlor trick). That's all well and good, but the real deal is using AI to determine something that can't be done quickly or perfectly using existing technology. For example: assessing the creditworthiness for people who don't have any credit (like many in the Gen Z and Millennial generations), or having it figure out what a creditworthy person looks like, even when their FICO score is demonstrably low. Sadly, these are not trivial undertakings, and they require skilled operators to setup and use the software—particularly if they're counting on it to make important decisions like credit scoring.

There are two main challenges with people, then. The first challenge is getting institution-wide buy-in from everyone. Company-wide support is a big motivator. The second challenge is the same as it's always been: supply and demand for talent. For one, universities aren't turning out as many engineers as this market needs, and the ones who do graduate—especially the top talent—gravitate toward more lucrative opportunities: fintechs, major banks, and other competitive tech industries. As a result, the spectrum of AI products is developing faster in the fintech space than it is inside of any financial institution.

Not only that, but getting organizational buy-in from your people can be hard. There's serious inertia going on at some financial institutions in America. But if you're able to show them what AI can do, as well as what it's already done, then convincing them that AI is in the company's future might not be such a hurdle. Still, finding and hiring the right people will be very difficult. Hiring and developing an AI talent internally could be expensive, and the timeline for your AI success might be slow. With that in mind, it's worth looking into AI partnerships and vendors if you don't have significant resources to throw at AI projects.

I should note here that working on the cloud is a critical first step toward being AI-ready. Working with analytics is a close second step. If you aren't doing those, then treat them both as prerequisites! Now, if you're wondering about timing (timing is everything, after all), you have four major variables to consider.

1. To stay on the cutting edge of technology and see the competitive advantages that AI brings, you need to get started on your first AI project a few years ago. Or, yesterday. Or, if you don't have a time machine, then start as soon as possible.

2. If you want your AI project(s) to succeed, you need to ensure that your institution is ready for it. You need buy-in from the board down, all the way to the end users. You and your institution must be AI-first.

3. You need to look into what tools are available. I can't provide an exhaustive list because the technology is progressing so rapidly that six months from this book's publication date, my recommendations could be outdated. Nevertheless, there are many inexpensive avenues to AI, any of which could be right for you.

4. You need the right people. Until humanity creates AGI—artificial general intelligence— you'll need forward-thinking programmers, data scientists, or other expert-level operators to work with your ANI models so that they give you the results you're looking for.

With those four considerations in mind, you can probably find an AI timeline that works best for you. If you don't have the resources to get past the second consideration, that doesn't mean that there is no good time for you to enter the AI marketplace; rather, it means that if you want to pursue AI, you should pursue it through partnerships rather than in-house development. (This will be the best option for most financial institutions.)

Now, for any institution looking to outsource their AI solutions, they might wonder: is this our AI? Is this our technology? These questions are just the tip of the iceberg when it comes to the ownership of AI.

Who Should Own AI?

As AI develops and solves more and more problems, governments, societies, companies, and individuals will struggle to answer, "who should own AI?" Just like the generational divides in how Baby Boomers, Gen X, Millennials, and Gen Z view social media, privacy, and our interactions with computers, AI furthers the debate in many ways.

Let's explore why this is such a big subject. To start, AI isn't a product in and of itself. Nobody's buying AI just to have it—they're buying it because it's a tool that helps them create a product or facilitate a service. It's the means to an end. The way I see it, AI is a product or service as much as "the wheel" is. Yes, you can buy a wheel, but nobody owns the design. Yes, you can use a wheel, but it's not going to do much on its own. What you make with the wheel is the product: a car, a bike, a wheelbarrow, or a train. The wheel just facilitates completion of the final result. Perhaps a more appropriate comparison would be programming language: could anyone truly make the argument that the inventor of Javascript or Python owns any of the products that they were used to create? AI is just a tool, a component, or a technique used to accomplish a greater goal. Thus, AI itself can't exactly be owned.

Also, many AI platforms are open source. Many of the biggest companies have open sourced their AI. Here some examples:

Amazon Alexa

Google's TensorFlow

Facebook's personal Assistant (Facebook M)

Microsoft's Computer Network Tool Kit

As long as you're on the cloud, all of these are available for use by your credit union, bank, or fintech. Even DARPA (the research arm of the department of defense) has open-sourced its tech. All of these people understand that the more people use their technology, the stronger their platforms will be in long term.

Other AI platforms, just like their open-source counterparts, are just that: platforms. They are, in effect, toolboxes. If you borrow a friend's toolset to build a table, does your friend own that table? Certainly not. But what if they also provided the screws and could take them back whenever they wanted? Let's say

Google decides Tensorflow shouldn't be open source, or they decide to put new constraints on what you're allowed to do with their platform. Who really owns your AI then?

Another issue is that AI is only in its nascent stages now. As I've shown earlier in this book, this early stage may not last long. What happens when ANI becomes AGI? Or, what happens when AGI become SAI? Would anyone feel comfortable owning a super-intelligent, even conscious thing? Worse yet, what happens if we accidentally build SkyNet? There are many schools of thought, here. Some believe that the best defense is to have multiple AI sources and competing AI to keep each of them in check. Some believe we should control it at the societal or governmental level.

I certainly don't have answers to these questions. I'm not sure anyone does. Yet, so long as we're thinking about AI, we might as well think about the challenges it will present. And fortunately, we're still pretty far off from these problems. We won't need answers anytime too soon.

For now, one of the greatest challenges we face with AI is the accelerating pace of change that it will bring. A company just one year ahead of another on the AI journey could be ahead by light years, developmentally. That is to say, the time between the two companies is relatively short, but the distance between them would be massive. That's because the exponential rate of progress for the first company would put them far ahead on the parabolic curve of computing power and capabilities.

That brings up concerns about single companies or individuals monopolizing AI. Imagine a financial institution with an AI so advanced that they build a 25% basis point advantage. Okay, that's manageable. But what if that advantage increases to a 50%, then a 100%, and then a 300% basis point advantage within a short period of time? Other banks and credit unions couldn't compete. In the past, if you saw a competitor with an advantage, you could study their service, their branches, and their products in order to make adjustments to your own. But if their proprietary AI is further developed than yours, what could you do? The accelerating returns on their AI progress would put them in position for a complete takeover of their industry (and maybe others as well).

One thing is for certain: keeping AI in the hands of the few could be disastrous for almost everyone else.

Finding ethical ways of democratizing access to it will safeguard our industry—and possibly humanity—against many forms of AI-based tyranny.

At this point, there are more questions than there are answers. Still, it's important to ask them. The more questions we ask, the closer we get to understanding what's at stake. And, if the right people hear the questions, the closer we get to answering them.

So, who owns AI? Nobody. Everybody. The platform providers. The developers, researchers, and scientists. The companies that design and built it.

But just in case you'd like more questions to ponder, I'll leave you with these:

Who should control AI?

What are the strengths and weaknesses of open-sourcing AI platforms?

What are the dangers and benefits of proprietary AI?

Could a bank or credit union think of itself as a platform?

Is your value in facilitating use of the platform by members, consumers, and businesses?

Are financial institutions controlled environments where they make all the rules? Or are they beholden to a greater set of rules?

When you think about using AI to improve your financial institution, do your goals or attitudes around it change depending on how you view your business model?

What limits, if any, should be placed on AI technology in this industry?

12

WHERE YOUR FINANCIAL INSTITUTION CAN GET STARTED WITH AI

I mentioned that I can't give a definitive list of resources for AI because it would be outdated so quickly. However, there are a few AI platforms that appear well-positioned for longevity. Throughout the course of this book, I've mentioned several of them in my case studies.

Don't worry, though—this chapter isn't about how to use the platforms. Rather, I'll suggest several areas where your financial institution might consider exploring AI solutions. These will be areas of your business in which AI has a very high potential of offering major rewards.

There are many examples of AI usage in the case studies I presented earlier, but those companies are already years ahead in development. They also may not be an exact fit for your needs. You know your institution's pain points better than anyone—it's possible that you could create a more effective, appropriate AI solution than they have. The following suggestions are a good starting point for your own custom-fit solution.

Contrarily, there are fintechs that address issues present in any of the following areas. Partnering with them could save you dramatic time, money, effort, and headaches. The work on your end would be about preparing for AI, rather than developing it. Either way you do it, you're set up to be AI-first.

Everyone's path to this industry is a little different, so everyone will bring their own ideas and sensibilities about how to solve the problems that we so frequently face. I like to draw from my experiences outside of the financial industry, too. When I think about which processes can be improved, I don't think only of processes unique to financial institutions—I think of pain points across industries.

For example, my first job was at a Taco Bell. Even in the 90s, they had streamlined the operation so that it didn't take many employees to keep the place running. But the Taco Bell of my kids' future will have half the employees (or less) than the one I worked at. Over the past ten years alone, the number of employees it takes to make your tacos has dropped by a couple per store.

It isn't hard to imagine where Taco Bell might cut labor requirements. While human-to-human interaction is still standard now, with improvements to NLP, we may soon see human-to-computer interactions. Asking for a "bean burrito minus red sauce" won't actually require a human, and we've already figured out how to pay for things on our own without cashiers to take our cards or cash for us.

Verbal NLP transactions will drastically change the environment. Even if things don't accelerate exponentially with AI, the productivity per employee per location will continue to expand and improve. Add in a touch of automation, and suddenly, what once took ten people will take only three. In Taco Bell, we'll see auto-filled drinks and auto-cooked fries. The modern fast food establishment is a balance of capital vs. productivity. So too will be finance.

This section will be full of many ideas. Some of these ideas are currently attainable—or will be in a year or two. Others are still very futuristic. However, because the pace of technological progress is accelerating, it's not a bad idea to think pretty far ahead. Big ideas can drive the small ones.

Teller Line

Just as with the fast food line, teller lines in branches are ripe with opportunities for AI improvement. A good deal of teller interactions could be automated with the help of AI. I can think of a whole ecosystem revolving solely around the teller line.

Immediately upon walking into a branch, a credit union's AI-based facial recognition system could detect the member, validate their identity, and queue up their information on the next available teller or member service representative. In addition, pattern recognition could pre-stage the member's prior and favorite transactions. Simultaneously, AI would calculate the value of the member and perform a series of predictive analytics to determine risk, propensity to refer, next product to sell, and customize fee and policy schedules. All of this would take place within the time it takes the member to walk across the lobby and get in line.

When the member finally reaches the teller, they might interact with an AI-enabled self-service kiosk. Their teller might not be a teller at all—or at least, not a human one.

Call Center

Call centers require a good deal of human labor, which is both expensive and error prone. That makes call centers an easy target for AI improvement. Here are a few ideas about how the call center of the future might look.

As members call in, they are verified by voice recognition and their accounts are analyzed. If the caller is feeling particularly vexed, the AI will determine human stress and emotion more accurately than humans can today, and it will adjust itself and its responses to suit. That kind of immediate insight could help financial institutions better understand the needs of their members, and it may help them build stronger relationships.

An AI-based call center could also understand requests in their native language. They might say, "transfer 50 from checking to savings," or "pay Verizon 143 bucks from my checking account on June 12th," and the AI could handle it. Aside from fulfilling almost any banking need, it could also help direct callers to additional resources, if required.

If AI continues at its current pace, it's conceivable that customers might have their AI assistants make the call for them; the AI assistant could pass the authentication and carry out any requests on the customer's behalf. It would be AI-to-AI calling! Or, for financial institutions that still use human call center staff, the staff may end up speaking with consumer AI without knowing it!

Collections

There are numerous areas where AI can aid in collections. Some of the low-hanging fruit is obvious: finding who is most likely to pay, knowing when to call, using AI to call or send reminders, debt negotiation, customer service, debt management, and more. These are all useful considerations, to be sure. Still, AI also gives us the chance to think outside the box.

I recently came across a company that has a network of repossession agents. Each tow truck is equipped with a license plate scanner. As they drive around, they catalog all the places they see account holders" cars. Need to find one for repossession? Just enter the VIN, and their database automatically determines the current license plate, calculates the odds of finding the vehicle at each location where the member lives, works, shops, etc., and alerts a repossession agent with an Uber-style map. AI can also analyze the images over time to determine whether the car is damaged before it gets back to the credit union.

There are many possibilities with AI in collections. As with Big Brother for car repossessions above, some of those possibilities are very different form your standard AI-enabled options.

Credit Scoring

If you took all of your financial institution's loan performance data and fed it into a machine learning algorithm, what patterns would it detect? What if you added to that algorithm every member communication, from the call center, to email, to Facebook, and even Yelp ratings?

Grain and QCash showed that AI can handle credit scoring by incorporating different kinds of data to paint a clearer picture of a borrower's ability to repay. And what if AI could prefill credit applications, conduct extensive analytics, and determine the odds of default more accurately? What if this new system could reduce the loan application time down to seconds instead of minutes or days?

Mortgage Loans

Just like with credit scoring, mortgage loans are a prime candidate for AI improvement. The AI system of tomorrow will be able to make better mortgage lending decisions through complex analytics. Then, it will be able to complete the application, gather all of the documentation, including appraisals, tax returns etc. AI could use image recognition to validate files, detect fraud, find anomalies, and prepare everything to be funded within a day.

With AI, mortgages won't take 30–60 days. The mortgage industry should look forward to same-day closings with less labor. The speed with which computers can complete tasks might make mortgages nearly instantaneous. Plus, when taking human loan officers out of the equation, AI-based mortgage lenders may benefit from reduced bias, which could affect many population segments.

Fee Income

Financial institutions make a lot of money from fees. While the extra income certainly helps the bottom line, those fees can frustrate and anger members, who feel nickeled-and-dimed to death. Sometimes, those fees can cost the institution more than they cost the member.

Caller dissatisfaction could lead them to leave for a competing bank or credit union. Often, customer service representatives reverse the fees, and the institution ends up losing time and money in the effort to placate their unhappy account holders.

With machine learning, we could potentially spot which fees should and shouldn't be reversed. It could fairly and consistently charge, refund, or adjust fees for every member, and it would do it automatically, with no representative time wasted.

Fraud Detection

I've already listed some examples in the book relating to fraud detection, but it's a big subject. In fact, it's one that indirectly affects many consumers' banking experiences. Fraud detection is especially necessary for credit card transactions. Typically, higher fraud rates occur during card-not-present transactions. However, there are some cases in which the card is present. It's rarer, but it's still a thing.

Some companies, like FlexPay, reduce fraud by analyzing broad swaths of consumer data to determine which transactions are legitimate and which aren't. Such complex analysis isn't really possible without machine learning. AI may thus curtail fraud by helping us better understand consumer behaviors.

Still, there are other kinds of fraud, and they can be harder to detect. Neural networks that process visual data could authenticate users, cards, and suspicious activity even when there is a card present. Machine learning could significantly increase fraud detection efficacy by sifting through massive amounts of ancillary data to ensure transactional authenticity.

Tools and Strategies at Your Disposal

You might be thinking, "okay, I see where I might implement AI in my financial institution. What are some specific examples of the tools I might use?"

As you probably guessed, there are several. I'll sort a few use cases into categories that may just spark your imagination.

One tool or strategy is optimization, which is the name of the game for machine intelligence. We know what kind of outcomes we want from our data, but traditional methods aren't getting us there—they're only getting us close. Machine learning reduces inefficiencies and allows nuance back into our equations. Here are a couple AI use cases that could help with product and pricing optimization.

For example, gesture control tracks user movements. Typically, it's been an easy way to interface with computers without relying on speech, text, or other traditional inputs. Essentially, it's like playing charades with a computer (which, if you can imagine, is already much easier than trying to play charades with my children). For instance, the Xbox Kinect allowed players to use their bodies as controllers. Motion and position sensors tracked body movement and translated it to the screen. It was a flashy but unwieldy accessory. Other forms of gesture control are more widespread and intuitive. For example, most smartphones (and smartphone games) rely on touch-based gesture control for navigation and control. Want to slice fruit in Fruit Ninja? That swipe is a gesture.

The ability for gesture control to "read" non-linguistic human input opens a lot of possibilities. Imagine being able to measure different types of user activity and engagement by tracking gestures, eye movement, or even body language. Think of what kind of insights you could gain from such minute observations.

Plus, reading human intention and emotion through gestures is an area rich with possibility. But so is pricing optimization. What if your rates, fees, terms, etc. on all of your financial products were dynamic or demand-based? (Uber and Lyft already take advantage of this with surge pricing.)

Machine learning and AI will allow pricing to be dynamically configured and set to maximize capacity, efficiency, asset/liability policies, loan policies etc. It won't take months or days to adjust things—instead, it will be optimized and delivered in real time. Pricing would be almost like the stock market, inasmuch as pricing could be notoriously unpredictable, but fair based on demand.

One of the ideas that I'm driving at with AI optimization is personalization. Let me paint a picture of why personalization is so important: I can't count how many times I've been asked to sign a petition or listen to a stranger's spiel while they canvas an area. I also don't know how often I've been cold-called—especially during dinner. And commercials during a streaming movie? Don't get even get me started! Nobody wants to deal with ads or sales pitches for irrelevant products or services. If I'm shopping for a house, then I want mortgage loan ads, not offers for new balance transfer credit cards. Personalized recommendations are one more area where machine learning really shines.

Personalization means staying relevant and understanding what people want and need will ensure that your financial institution can continue to provide value to your customers, increasing their loyalty to you. Additionally, this engine will help you push your offers across multiple channels: email, website, online and mobile banking, and so on.

Of course, those communications don't mean much if they aren't sent where (or when) their target can see them. Thus, marketing and communications are another area ready for AI improvement. There are ways to personalize experiences and track marketing ROI, but many are unsophisticated, and they don't always work the way we hope. In many instances, people rely on educated guesswork to know where and when to feature their marketing assets. AI offers a bit more certainty with digital placement.

Oh yeah, and then there's product information management. AI can monitor branches, websites, email engagement, and social activity. With the information it gathers, it can tweak or revise product and service information across all distribution points as needed. The impact on compliance will be huge when you can update once, and then let AI change everything else to fit.

This kind of self-editing has bigger implications for marketing and website personalization, too. AI could enable seamless integration with language, geography, color preferences, and so on, tailoring images and messaging to individual customer sensibilities. Instead of pre-built dynamic landing pages, imagine an entire website that changes language, appearance, and more, all depending on the user. Same product, different viewer preferences. What better way to make people feel understood and engaged?

Allowing AI to understand visual content is important for more than just advertisement. It also helps with visual search capability, which may be increasingly important as more visual content makes its way onto the web. By some predictions, 80% of all consumed internet content will be video-based. Imagine searching the net using pictures or video instead of text or voice recognition.

If that sounds far-fetched, think again. Already, people use apps like Shazam to help them search for songs. Shoppers in grocery or electronics stores might snap a picture of a product to compare prices on Newegg or Amazon. Websites, products, and content will need machine learning and AI to help consumers find the right information and products. (Don't worry—by then, they'll be able to reliably tell chihuahua and blueberry muffins apart.)

Finding images on the internet could be easier with better categorization. AI-based image tagging could handle that task. Plus, image tagging is usually a tedious manual affair; machine learning and automation could take that burden off someone else's shoulders and do a better job tailoring the image tags for searches. For example, algorithms could tag and contextualize images to improve search engine optimization (SEO) and visibility. After training the computer to recognize relevant search terms and popular nomenclature, it could generate accurate, germane image descriptions that stem from consumer language rather than financial jargon.

Optimized Marketing Communications

You may have noticed that many of these ideas share a theme. Optimizing marketing communication may just be the culmination of that theme.

There's no reason to shout your message into an anonymous crowd anymore. Data and AI give us the tools we need to identify and locate qualified leads. This intelligent targeting costs less and works better. And this isn't even cutting-edge! Tools like Appzen and Phrasee have been around for a while now. Appzen tracks customer behavior across devices, so sales knows when and where to start a conversation. Phrasee suggests personalized NLP messages to ensure that members and customers receive fewer "marketing-" or "robotic-sounding" messages. It's easy to bring this technology into your financial institution.

RE: Data Tracking

Sometimes traditional marketing techniques like commercials and print ads just feel old-timey and outdated now, like street vendors shouting at thronged masses, touting the benefits of their wonder elixirs and snake oils. Optimized marketing communication is more about finding the right audience and reminding them you exist. Rather than shouting to the masses, you can speak personally to people who have, knowingly or otherwise, indicated that they're interested in your products.

Having a better idea about how to reach prospective clients, members, and customers gives any marketing department a leg up. In the future, neuromarketing could corral the information necessary to get that advantage. Here's how: credit unions and banks may leverage neuroscience and biometric sensors to understand how their content affects emotions and memory. Marketing efforts could be targeted to reach people when they're most receptive to messaging—and most able to remember it. You could virtually guarantee that your content has the intended effect.

Of course, all the receptivity in the world doesn't mean a thing if you can't bring in context. Context-aware marketing would ensure that marketing efforts are relevant. There would be few things worse than offering a student loan the day after your customer's kid gets a college rejection letter. Context-aware marketing leverages machine vision and NLP to help provide context for where you place ads or content.

One potential roadblock to these kinds of capabilities is in data quantity and quality. AI and machine learning are data hungry—they get more accurate results when they have access to more data. Financial institutions need more outside data to validate assumptions and create tailored experiences. Relying solely on in-house data might not provide the kind of robust data set that machine learning needs in order to facilitate the meaningful insights that neuromarketing and context-aware marketing require. Third-party partnerships or data would be essential for getting any of these ideas off the ground in the near future.

Now, if you want to improve marketing communications, you have to consider channel-specific optimizations. There are different ways of approaching different digital communication avenues and knowing the differences between them is key.

AI can create and deliver customized messages based on users' mobile behavior. Many consumers—particularly those from younger generations—have their phones with them at all times. Optimizing your mobile marketing experience means putting your most relevant messages in their hands and pockets at all times.

Mobile pathways aren't the only digital avenues for marketing outreach, of course. Email marketing has been around for decades now, so it's easy to forget that it's still effective. Still, it could be made even more effective. AI can customize your email messaging to individual behavior. You can detect which email type performs better with your product and customer, essentially performing constant A/B testing. Customization should at the very least include email structure, images, and timing, but it might also tailor content, frequency, and more.

If it sounds like too much work to do "constant A/B testing" with emails, then boy do I have news for you. (You know where this is going, I'm sure.) AI in the future will be able to generate content that is unique and fluid for your audience. There already exist tools that produce written work that is virtually indiscernible from human-generated content.

Less impressively, there are already "article spinners," which are programs that analyze content and then produce a slightly altered version for redistribution. These tools help people create dozens of usable drafts of the same basic blog or article. At this point, we have the technology to create content and then make variations of it. Using AI for content generation is just around the bend.

Let's not forget though: your messages to members and customers are only half the communications equation. The other half is their feedback to you. In-branch feedback and surveys are common communications, but not all customer feedback is explicit. For example, social media interaction is a form of customer feedback. If your institution tweets and receives an average of 1,000 likes and 100 retweets, you've got a baseline to work with. If a new tweet gets 100 likes and 10 retweets, that might tell you something. Analyzing every form of feedback can help you understand what people think about you—and if you're in danger of losing accounts.

But let's say you do find something amiss. One of your customers or members isn't happy about something, and they want to speak with customer service. This is your opportunity to win them back. You could optimize your customer service to identify which customers to contact, how to respond to them, or to automatically assign them to the right agent. Or, speaking of the right agent, what if you could implement intelligent call routing? You could route calls to the best-fit customer service agent by matching customer profiles with agent specialty or historical performance.

Plus, if you could reduce some of a caller's irritation before they even speak to someone, that could make things even easier. By using voice authentication, callers wouldn't have to jump through a series of authentication hoops just to prove they are who they say they are. They could begin addressing their problem right away.

Finally, customer service response suggestions could assist agents on calls. They could listen in, providing best-practice answers and ideas for how to solve customer problems. They could also indicate appropriate times to upsell or cross-sell.

Dreaming Big vs
Staying Grounded

Some of the suggestions above are still a few years out. Some are just now entering the realm of possibility. That could be discouraging to financial institutions that are looking for slam-dunk AI projects. If what your want are a few easy wins, then a better starting place for AI development might be with some of the other use cases earlier in the book. For example, some aspects of marketing optimization, fraud prevention, call center assistance, or lending would be much easier to achieve in the short run.

But I don't want you to dream small. I want you to dream big. Because the fact of the matter is that some of my suggestions above aren't that far off. The next few years will bring some of these technologies and ideas to the fore. Would you rather watch your competitors introduce these capabilities, or would you like to develop them yourself?

Yes, being part of the production of technology is difficult. It takes time, energy, expertise, patience, and a whole lot of creativity. And speaking of creativity, I will be the first to admit that I'm not always as creative as I'd like to be. My suggestions above are limited to what I could think of, but they are in no way exhaustive.

Ultimately though, balance is key. AI is a growing field, and it's dominating an increasing market share for many services. If you're ready for your AI journey, remember to balance your goals. Familiarize yourself with the technology by picking the low-hanging fruit. Get some easy wins under your belt.

But always remember that AI is the future as far as we can see it. Don't get so distracted by easy, obtainable goals that you forget to look further ahead. Give yourself a few difficult goals. Shoot for the moon. Even if you miss, you'll still be pretty far out there. Plus, the technology will catch up sooner than you might think. And when it does, you'll be on the cutting edge rather than struggling to catch up.

Don't think AI can write marketing materials for you? Don't get too cocky!

`OpenAI, an AI project from Tesla's Elon Musk and Y Combinator's Sam Altman, debuted an AI text-generation bot in early 2019. It created credible, realistic articles, blogs, and press releases using groundbreaking new text generation techniques.

They never released it publicly. It was too powerful and too convincing. OpenAI researchers feared that it could be used to spread misinformation, undermine elections, unfairly influence products through reviews, and so on. A far less powerful version is available for people to play with; even the tamed version is impressive.

RE: AI-generated marketing

13

HOW AI WILL IMPACT YOUR PEOPLE

Although this book is about AI in finance, we can't forget who implements that AI and who benefits from it: people. All the attempts in the world to change will fall flat if nobody wants or believes in that change. Finding the right people, from the experts, to the everyday employees, to the end users is key to bringing about the kind of change you want to see. But the end users already want AI. Are you and your organization prepared to give it to them?

As management consultant Peter Drucker said, "culture eats strategy for lunch." One of the hardest things to change in any organization is culture. Often, we mistakenly think that human resources departments can change culture. They can't. They can only moderate it. The reality is that culture is a sum of parts—in this case, the parts are the people who work or volunteer at the financial institution. Together, their collective wisdom, decision making, teamwork, and styles create the corporate culture. If their culture and their attitudes toward technology can't change, then neither can the financial institution, regardless of any overarching strategy.

I've seen this resistance to technological change firsthand. I was hired as a teller in my first credit union job, and within days, I was moved to data processing (now IT). I was assigned two tasks: first, I had to deploy Windows PCs into a dumb terminal environment. Second, I was to teach everyone how to use a mouse. I was thrilled. Someone was actually going to pay me to install computers and teach people to use them. I had grown up working with computers so it would be a cinch.

I was practically curled up in a corner and crying just a week later. People couldn't even find the cursor, let alone tell the difference between single- and double-clicks on the mouse. There was a massive gap in computer knowledge to be overcome, and the people learning from me just wanted to go back to what they knew best even though they knew it would be faster and more efficient in the long run. As I continued trying to teach people things (such as how to change toner cartridges), I realized that most employees resisted learning how to do things themselves. Instead, they wanted to make any new information, technology, or tools someone else's problem. They wanted business as usual, but with me managing all the tricky computer stuff that they were afraid of. They wanted to have their cake and eat it too.

It was frustrating back then, but today, the stakes are even higher. In the financial world, organizations live or die based on their ability to update, innovate, and change rapidly. We must keep up with other businesses, or they could soon overtake traditional banking models as we know them. The problem is that we haven't developed that sense of urgency—we haven't made it integral to our culture. We're being held back by the members of our teams—or even the members of our industry—who are the most resistant to technological progress.

The leap from our current state of technology to AI, including AGI, will be faster and more challenging to adjust to than even the PC and internet revolutions. Scarier still, the stakes for this leap are high. That goes not only for our industry, but for humans and the future of labor as a whole. Sure, productivity will increase, and laborers can accomplish more work with less effort each day, but *how* we work—what we do, how we do it, and what we think about it—will change drastically. Work in the future may be unrecognizable (and possibly unavailable).

The question is, are we ready for this change? Can we take this leap? Are we prepared for progress of this magnitude? Some people are, and they're building it into their corporate culture. Others aren't, and they already wonder why their business isn't moving forward and adapting quickly to change.

Culture—the people, decisions, data, and ideas that flow through an organization every day—is the driving factor in progress and innovation. Every day in credit unions and banks, people make millions of decisions. Some of them are small: should we refund a fee? Should we approve a new account? Other decisions are potentially massive and can alter the fates of account holders: should we approve this car loan?

Should we offer this mortgage? Should our organization approach banking differently and offer new services to our account holders, such as mobile and online banking?

This kind of strategic planning comes from the people who have been empowered to make these decisions. In time, both on a granular level and through volume, they steer institutional cultures in the appropriate directions. With ANI at our doors, we stand at the brink of an AI revolution. What decision will we make? Do we accept it? Or do we call AI a trend or a parlor trick? Do we ignore it until it's too late?

And if we do embrace AI, what decisions to we allow it to make? As I've shown, we already trust it with a lot. Some AI has gone from bleeding-edge technology to standard feature almost overnight. In many respects, what ANI currently offers isn't revolutionary. Rather, it's more about automating difficult or tedious tasks, optimizing workflows or outreach, or finding better, more accurate ways of doing things (such as improving credit or payment models). That's not revolutionary so much as it is common sense. What is revolutionary is how we think about it: how we approach it, work with it, and deploy it.

If you want to know which of your competitors use AI now, look no further than JP Morgan Chase. A couple years ago, Chase debuted its Contract Intelligence (COIN) program—a machine learning system that reviews documents, interprets loan agreements, and so forth. COIN was an immediate success; it replaced about 360,000 legal and accounting hours per year, many of which resulted from human error on small tasks. COIN finished that work in seconds. They achieved buy-in for their AI by assigning those workers higher-order tasks. That's a lot of hours freed up for non-drudgework.

You may think that the culture of JP Morgan Chase doesn't translate to your financial institution. In many ways, you're right. It probably can't. It's a juggernaut bank with more money tied up in in-house technological development than most financial institutions have in assets. Nevertheless, their success suggests that AI has a necessary place in our industry. It also indicates that the culture in our industry can change—and that for some, it already has changed. We're not talking about the future—we're talking about now.

Changing Culture, Changing People

I've heard many objections to shifting institutional culture to be AI-first. They usually sound something like this:

"It won't happen for a while."

"The technology isn't there yet."

"We don't know where to start."

"We don't have the resources."

"We don't want to be the first ones to do it—we want to know what works."

"It's always worked this way, so there's no need to change."

You may have even heard one of your teammates say one of these phrases. Heck, maybe you uttered these words yourself. That's fine, but only under one condition: you must admit that these objections are rooted in fear and misunderstanding. They are not rooted in practice or reality.

There's an exercise that I've introduced in a few strategic planning sessions now. I call it "What If?" The goal is to get people to stop thinking about what's holding them back either personally or as an institution, and instead to get them thinking about what other people or institutions might accomplish in the same period of time. This allows people to think about what is possible without asking them to be responsible for that change. When other, unnamed experts are the ones in charge of innovation, people entertain more optimistic scenarios regarding their industry's capacity to effect change.

When I start the "What If" exercise, I start simply. I ask them what has changed in the last ten years. As a group, they identify major developments in the world and in their financial institutions. We list and analyze the rise of technologies like cryptocurrencies, cloud computing, mobile banking, and machine learning. This part of the exercise shows them how quickly they've already adapted to emerging technological developments.

Then, I have the group grapple with a hypothetical: imagine ten years in the future. Same group, same institution, different decade. I ask them what they think will be different.

There are a few key areas I ask the group to concentrate on. What kinds of technology will emerge? Which technologies will become standard? How will those technologies impact their account holders? How do they impact their jobs and daily operations? How can they prepare for these possibilities?

Of course, I welcome developments outside of the financial industry as well. More often than not, the most groundbreaking ideas come from relatively unrelated fields. (Think, for example, about what we have or might take from gaming: virtual reality, image and content generation, gamification, rewards, etc.)

Usually, this part of the exercise highlights a group's pessimism about their own progress, capabilities, or capacity to change. Critically though, it highlights their optimism about what other companies or financial institutions might accomplish over the same period. Sometimes when I point this out, I can see the little "aha!" moment that people have. A few see that their objections to their own ability to innovate are rooted in their culture. It's not that they can't accomplish similar things—rather, they've told themselves that it's not part of their job to look ahead and go beyond the status quo.

After they think about what would change in ten years, I ask about what might be different in five years. Finally, I ask what might change in one year, or even the next week.

When I do this exercise, we quickly identify patterns and potential bottlenecks. We also see opportunities to go faster along the way. The real beauty of the exercise is in the process, though. By asking a group about the future—one year, five years, ten—I ask them to actively change their thoughts. Instead of worrying about daily operations and activities, I ask them to be forward-thinking. I get them to think like innovators. There's no better way to prepare people for change than to make them to think about it. Any shift in culture starts with a change in mindset and imagination.

What Kind of People Will It Take?

I'm not saying that I'm a perfect example of what kind of person it will take. I'm not. However, I do have experience doing many things in this industry. The position I hold today, and much of my expertise, comes from facing new challenges head on and being willing to adapt to them.

During my first banking job in high school, I remember how manual all of the processes were. We did everything with a 10-key calculator, and batching debit and credit cards was a nightmare. I could hardly stand it. I knew there was a better way, though—thinking differently about the process was key. I wrote some Turbo Paschal software to automate new student bank applications on an IBM XT. I printed the approved applications at the end of the day and took them to our sponsor bank. It saved me a ton of time and paperwork. Our student bank opened over a hundred new accounts, while the other two in the region each opened about dozen.

My emerging technology dramatically improved the onboarding process of my high school bank. We saw that improvement not because the technology was there—it had been for a while—but because someone was willing to make it work.

Foremostly then, the kind of person you need to help you create AI solutions is someone who is willing to apply the technology that already exists to the purposes you need. If you want to skip the vendors and build your own AI solutions, then you'll need to either hire an expert (or a team of experts) or you'll need to grow your own AI person. Hiring experts is pretty straightforward. Growing your own? That's harder. Still, there are two main ways that you grow your own AI developer.

Option one: hire someone who knows something about AI straight out of high school or college. Give them real problems to solve and see what happens. It's a cheap investment, and they may surprise you. Plus, they'll help you see what's coming and how best to prepare for it.

Option two: pick the person or people in your institution who learn the fastest. Give them the tools they need to learn, play around, explore, and experiment. Don't lock them up in a closet somewhere away from the other departments—keep them connected and empower them to disrupt the processes that are most ready for change.

Who Else Will You Need?

Changing culture is not an easy task. Your people must be ready for it. Your current employees will need to be ready for a future that looks much different than the present. Your future employees will need different sets of skills than the ones your current employees trained for.

With the coming of AI, each area of financial institutions will be impacted differently. Consequently, it is important not only to look for patterns among each person, but also among each department. Any major cultural shift toward becoming AI-first will require three kinds of people: the nimble, the curious, and the self-taught.

The nimble folks will be essential, as the rules of the game will change quickly. The curious will think about the ways to take advantage of the opportunities that present themselves, and they will find those opportunities without even looking. The self-taught will be essential due the constantly changing environment, the new ways to do things, and shifting customer expectations.

Technology jobs will change. Why hire programmers when AI will program faster and with less error? Instead, we'll need jobs that emphasize creativity, strategy, and direction. Our technologists will need to get better at finding data, defining problems and limits, and working across departments.

Human resources will change. AI will find, recruit, profile, and sort resumes to help find better fits for jobs. AI may do the interviewing for us. Algorithms can sort through hundreds of resumes, applications, and video interviews for key skills, insights, and problem-solving capabilities.

Everyone will have an assistant. Mundane tasks will be automated. People will have time to spend on more dynamic, higher order work.

Jobs of the future will require skills that AI can't replicate as well. These skills may include creativity, empathy, and compassion. Basically, we'll need to prioritize and develop that which makes us human.

These are non-transactional jobs. Most customer service representatives spend 90% of their efforts on transactional tasks: data entry, opening new accounts, approving loans, and so forth. These representatives are often overworked and underappreciated. What's more, the work is exceedingly tedious, as they might occasionally need to reenter the same data in multiple systems. Currently we expect representatives to open accounts, enroll users in online banking, order checks, and interact with dozens of systems to do their jobs. In the future, AI will take over much of that work, enabling these employees to build more impactful relationships and solve bigger problems for our customers and members.

This more personal kind of work reaches beyond just entry-level work and extends to even the C-level players. For years, our organizational structure has been aligned in a top-down manner. That is, you more often hear the question, "who do you work for?" and not "who do you work with?" Employees in an AI-enabled world will need to be good at communication and collaboration. Instead of organizing for efficiency and efficacy (that's AI's job), institutions will have to organize for agility and adaptability.

Agility and adaptability also mean speed, and speed doesn't exactly make our industry comfortable. With more speed comes more risk. But with AI, that's okay. The machines do the calculations, which removes a considerable amount of risk. It's only the ideas, thought processes, and innovation that need to come quickly. Fortunately, there are a few ways to manage the growing pace of change.

Embrace the speed of change. Spend time thinking about which functions could move more quickly. Try to understand your own customer and member expectations when working with other industries. Look at the impacts that digital transformation has had in other industries as well as our own, and then draw inspiration from those successes.

Intentionally move positions. Executives should move through multiple roles and disciplines so that they never get too comfortable. Comfortability breeds complacency and doesn't build new neural pathways or ways of thinking. When we get too comfortable, we stop learning. Introducing new people, thoughts, ideas, and ways of thinking can help us move and adapt more quickly.

Involve your employees. In groups, have them assess, analyze, and critique incentives, projects, and systems. This will get them used to more complex evaluation and analysis, leading to higher, more agile performance.

Review your workplace tools. Trello, Asana, Basecamp, Slack, Workplace, SweetProcess, and many others are designed to support agile workplaces, enhance communication, and help teams perform optimally. Do your tools help your team to move forward, or do they maintain existing, potentially outdated work patterns?

Adopt agile performance reviews. Once a year is not enough. Help your teams learn faster by giving more continuous feedback. A lot can get off track in a year, and many bad habits or shortcuts can develop faster than that. Keeping everyone on the same general track will keep things from straying too far away from your destination.

If you want to succeed with an agile workplace, you'll need to prioritize hiring employees that can adjust to changes in their workplace. Basically, the flexibility of your personnel will be more important than the speed of your technologies and processes. AI will be able to offer that kind of operational quickness. It will also be able to handle most administrative work and paper-pushing. People won't have to book appointments, set reminders, keep projects on track, or other things of that nature. Instead, in the near future, teams and people will need to focus on solving more complex problems like business strategy and relationship building.

One of the biggest fears that people have about AI and automation (aside from a robot uprising) is that they take people out of the equation. It's a valid concern, and it's not outrageous to worry that technology will make many jobs obsolete. But that fear rarely comes from a place of true understanding. Especially at this stage, most AI frees up employees to work on more important tasks. AI and automation move people to a different part of the equation.

The truth is that people are just as important as ever. Finding and training the right people will make your company culture—and by extension, your financial institution—better prepared to meet your members' and customers' diverse and changing needs.

To get started with AI, you'll need to change your culture. To continue with AI, you'll need to start to rethink labor as we know it. The future of banking depends on our adaptability.

14

SECURITY AND PRIVACY FOR AI

I moved from job to job in my early days in the industry. As I've made clear by now, the first bank I worked at didn't have the internet. Fraud and security prevention were accomplished through personal relationships. Tellers knew their customers, or they could check a signature card, check a driver's license, and cross their fingers. When a customer came in from another branch and the transaction was considered high risk, we had to have the primary branch fax the signature card over or talk to the primary branch manager for approval.

Those were the easy days of security and privacy. Then the internet came out, and things started getting more complicated. It presented a huge leap forward in how people interacted with their financial institutions—and how they could circumvent traditional security and privacy measures.

In my second banking job, I installed our first internet connection, created a website, and became customer number five at Digital Insight, one of the largest internet banking providers today. The dotcom boom raged on, and I moved on to Fiserv to build disaster recovery solutions for financial institutions. Shortly thereafter, I went into Y2K consulting for a bunch of credit unions. When that threat passed, I became the IT manager at a midsized credit union. By that time, I had a lot more experience under my belt, and I could see which direction things were heading: I was entering the wild, wild west of security and privacy.

Things were a mess at the credit union. They had an internet connection, but nobody knew the difference between a public and non-public IP address. If you were at home on AOL, you could literally enter in the

IP address of the credit union mainframe and boom! You were on the core system. Nobody really thought about security—everyone was so excited about the possibilities of a connected world that they forgot about the dangers of one.

Very quickly, the security craze began. It started with proxy servers with firewalls, and then came email and file servers. After malware started popping up, we began putting anti-virus software on our PCs. Next came firewall and password management. Each year we would add a few new security tools. These days, it takes teams of people, systems, policies, and procedures to prevent data breaches.

I bring up the past to contrast it with the present. Security and privacy are always major considerations in our industry, and they're getting stricter and more stringent by the year. There's a lot of money and personally identifiable information (PII) at play. That's enough reason to make anybody nervous. However, our security and privacy considerations can't always keep up with progress. I've seen this happen a few times throughout my career.

In 2013, I joined forces with the founder of Digital Insight, Paul Fiore, and we started CU Wallet: a mobile wallet allowing consumers to pay for everything with their phone. Then, ApplePay came out and we put everything on hold. It wasn't just that we were nervous about competition—usually we love it! But we also realized that security and compliance were going to be a minefield for the near future. To this day there is still little to no adoption of mobile wallets, and privacy concerns are part of that.

Mobile wallets thus highlighted an interesting issue: using cards—both debit and especially credit cards—carries a high fraud risk. Consequently, the mobile ecosystem had to evolve considerably to ensure it could protect the financial and personal information of its users. It struck me how complex security and privacy issues had gotten in such a short time. It used to be so much simpler!

At the same time, it seems that each generation cares less about privacy. On social media, users share a staggering amount of personal information over Snapchat, Facebook, Twitter, Instagram, LinkedIn, and even Google. The amount of personal and behavioral data that these services gather has already drawn public and legal attention—how can we safely protect people and ensure data security in our changing technological climate?

On the other hand, a user's willingness to share their information with Amazon, Google, Facebook, or Apple does confer benefits. Using one login to access multiple connected websites and apps adds to the sense of hyper-personalization and convenience that many consumers prefer.

Keeping in mind both sides of these coin—hyper-personalization and privacy, convenience and security—what does this mean for the future of AI? We're still struggling to catch up to the security concerns of the last decade. Are we ready for the security concerns of the next?

So, here's the thing: hyper-personalization is here to stay. Imagine if you logged onto Netflix and it gave you your mom's recommendations—you wouldn't be impressed. Yet, most banks and credit unions struggle to personalize the member journey. The number of systems it takes to deliver consumer loans, credit cards, debit cards, online banking, and every other service makes it difficult.

AI and machine learning will change that quickly. It will allow you to instantaneously aggregate and analyze all your customers' data and then adjust their banking experience to fit. Customers already expect this from their other consumer choices, and it won't be long until they expect it from their financial institutions as well. They will assume that if they talk to your call center, your branch manager will know and understand the problem a few days later.

To pull off this kind of hyper-personalization, financial institutions need to place bets today about providers who can get them there. Most of the companies working toward this today are startups. Choosing the right online banking provider is like trying to pick an adult heartthrob movie star based on their baby pictures. The venture capital world will place dozens of bets and hope that one of them pans out. Banks and credit unions don't have that luxury, but they do have influence: they're the ones with customers and end users. This gives financial institutions unique leverage to partner up or pool investments. All they need to do after they've made their choice is to hang on for a wild ride.

One of the first personalization issues you'll have to deal with is creepiness. It's already unsettling when I have a conversation about turntables and then my Instagram feed features audio gear from Best Buy five minutes later.

So, how much personalization is too much? Maybe AI can tell us. For one person, seeing personalized ads makes them feel understood, and they're thankful that they're not looking at products that have no relevance to their daily life. To another person, they try to figure out which of their apps is tracking them so they can delete it.

Financial institutions will have to find a way to walk this line. They will have to determine which aspects of hyper-personalization people find convenient and which they find creepy. A rough rule of thumb might be, "don't tip your hand about how much you know." If a couple just found out that they're expecting, it's probably not a good time to inundate them with ads for diapers and baby carriages. At least wait until they make it public!

Still, personalization does matter to people. For one, people like to be known. The same way people smile when the bartender greets them and knows how they like their old fashioneds, people smile when they don't have to show their ID four or five times just to deposit a check.

RE: Delta Airlines

Delta Airlines took this idea and ran with it—in Atlanta, Delta passengers can opt into biometric check-ins. Instead of showing their passport to everyone with a badge, they can show it only once and then let computers keep track of them the rest of the way. Sure, it raises even more privacy questions in airports, but it's also wildly convenient.

Financial institutions might draw inspiration from this approach. Removing repetition in data entry, security checks, etc. is a great place to start. Then, we can build on that trust to create amazing consumer experiences. And trust is the key word, here—trust comprises frequency, transparency, commonality, empathy, vulnerability, generosity, resiliency, and reciprocity. No one facet of trust can make it or break it—they all work together. Your personalization and data strategy must accommodate all aspects of trust. If your customers can't trust you, then they won't give you their data. If they won't give you their data, you can't deliver good experiences. The customer who doesn't trust you is as good as gone.

When you're building your AI solutions, keep trust in mind. You also need data. Good data is one of the first steps to building trust.

Here's what you can do:

> Get rid of irrelevant, outdated, or illegal data. If the data is five years old, it's useless. Personalization is about immediacy, not ancient history.

> Determine which data you need. I recommend small-scale testing and proving out algorithms in manual one-by-one modes until you can see patterns and improve things. Once you get this dialed in, you can better define problems and scale up with machine learning.

> Source additional data responsibly. Get your data from good sources and stay transparent about where you source it.

Once you have your data, you're ready to worry about higher-order AI security and privacy issues. Unfortunately, in the same way that it's hard to predict what SAI will be like, it's also hard to predict what kind of security issues will arise from ubiquitous ANI. Nevertheless, there are a few basic things to look out for.

Fraud will be a major issue. Today, smart criminals try things around the fringes. They fax in fake IDs, forge signatures, or steal credit cards or card numbers to run up charges.

Now, imagine that criminal has access to AI. The same way that AI and automation allow financial institutions to work more efficiently and with less error, it could allow criminals to do the same. Instead of scamming a few places, they could have algorithms scam hundreds or thousands of institutions at a time. Essentially, AI could allow criminals to scale their operations.

Cyberweapons are also a threat. Computers themselves could be weaponized more than they already are; powerful processing and AI algorithms can overwhelm most financial institutions. With proper targeting, the effects could be devastating. Phishing and farming scams could be more realistic—and hyper-personalized.

On the bright side, that same AI can be used defensively. It will be essential to develop heuristic solutions and AI tools to protect financial institutions from hacking threats. It may also be rather expensive, but maybe that's the price of progress.

Misinformation campaigns deserve a place on this list as well. Recent election events have shown just how influential fake news is on consumer behavior. How should financial institutions respond to disgruntled members or blackmailers who use misinformation campaigns to sway broader public opinion? AI could potentially create very realistic videos, sounds and voices, and news articles that would be difficult to validate. Even if these campaigns are caught, the damage could already be done.

Of course, these are just a few of the obvious ideas. There are many more creative ways to use AI unscrupulously. A financial institution could just be a casualty when it's used to conduct and internet of things (IOT) hack. An autonomous vehicle could run into a bank to rob it. A credit union be the victim of sophisticated spoofing to misdirect them from the real fraud right under their noses.

Security and privacy are almost philosophical concerns at this point. We barely understand the questions. And we may have answers, but we don't know if they're the right answers. Ten years from this book's publication, we might see a paradigm-changing use for AI that renders all this moot.

Of course, like many aspects of this book, it's difficult to discuss specifics. It's impossible to predict exactly what AI will look like, let alone how people will harness it. But a few things are for sure: computing power will increase, as will the benefits and dangers that come with it. The kinds of data that AI incorporates will expand as well, as will our comfort with what it does with that information. And AI technologies will grow stronger, giving both criminals and security teams new tools to work with.

We can also count on new regulations for security and privacy. Compliance may be a nightmare. If there's any consolation to the emerging compliance issues, it may be this: regulations will ensure the safety of all people as AI grows in prominence. It's a promising but potentially dangerous technology. We should all sleep better knowing that AI will be used for the betterment of humanity rather than its downfall.

Another possible consolation is this: though compliance may be a nightmare, it might at least be a very exciting nightmare. That's got to be worth something, right?

15

AI STRATEGY

———

Up until this chapter, I've spoken about a lot of hypotheticals. I've tried to paint a picture of where our industry has been, where it is now, and where it's going. With any luck, I've created a sense of urgency about the use of AI in the financial industry. More importantly, I hope that you've started thinking about your own pain points and how you might be able to address them—AI opens so many possibilities that it would be a shame not to think a little bigger than usual.

There are numerous ways to approach AI, but each institution has different needs. Keeping that need for individuality in mind, I can't outline specific strategies going forward. But still, you probably need some nuts and bolts. In this chapter, I'll try my best to provide a few of those nuts and bolts.

Preparing for AI isn't as easy as we'd like. We can't just send out a company-wide email to say, "prepare for AI!" or "we humbly welcome our new robot overlords!" Simply telling people that AI is on the horizon—and fast approaching—won't actually get much done. Yes, announcing intentions helps, but at some point, the big questions must get answered. (Or at least, we should begin asking them.)

Which big questions, you ask? How about these:

> What are our biggest needs, and which ones can be addressed with AI?
>
> Where do I start?
>
> What should my AI team look like?
>
> How do I determine an AI budget?
>
> How do I get buy-in?

The answer to the first question is the best starting point. It may influence the answers to the rest of the questions on the list.

So, what are your biggest needs? There's not much point in developing a solution for a problem you don't have just because it would be easy.

And which of those needs can be solved with AI? If your biggest problem is that your tellers are rude, then there may be some easier first steps to take that don't include AI development. (Then again, maybe it's time to jump ahead to some self-service kiosks...)

Answering the first question doesn't mean deciding what to solve or how to solve it! That comes later. The first step is getting the ideas flowing to make sure you're on track.

Until you answer those questions, you shouldn't even begin discussing which tools, which stack, or which vendors you'd want to use. However, once you've spent enough time discussing your needs and your capabilites, then you can look ahead.

Only then, when you have an idea about which area or areas could benefit the most from AI, are you truly ready to ask the next question...

Where Do I Start with AI?

Many organizations will start down this journey. However, many will get frustrated and their attempts will fail or get sidelined. **Here are some potential first steps:**

Step 1: Make a plan

Step 2: Don't leave it open ended—focus on solving actual business problems

Step 3: Make sure senior management is involved and on board

Step 4: Hire or develop the right talent

Let's examine each one in more depth.

Step one

When making a plan, I recommend starting with a pilot project. To begin, pick a few of the ideas you came up with during the first exercise and explore them in more detail. Brainstorm as many ideas and problems as you can. Don't worry about bad or silly ideas—you can throw those out soon. But write them down, or at least say them out loud, regardless of whether they're good. They may spur a better idea from a colleague.

When you've brained your last storm (or is it stormed your last brain?), it's time to evaluate your options. Assess your best ideas with a modified *pros* and *cons* list, looking instead for *impact* and *complexity*. The impact would be the range of benefits to your institution for various business departments, customers and members, employees, risk and compliance, marketing presence, margin, and so forth. The complexity would be how difficult the project would be to see through. If there's no similar solution on the market, it could take years of developmental work. Is the impact worth the complexity?

Step two

Make sure that your solution(s) deliver business value. Keep clearly defined business objectives, such as reducing attrition rates by 30%, growing business loans by 10%, or improving sales efficiency and marketing presence. You may even decide that your first goal is to develop a machine learning or NLP solution that performs as well as humans, but doesn't yet show marked improvement. That's okay! In the process, you will create a technology platform that has better scalability and room for improvement in the long run.

Finally, if possible, determine what kind of business unit support you can expect and estimate a time to delivery. That will give you a rough timeline to work with. Having a timeline isn't necessary, but it can help you and your team keep on track and work through inertia. Staying responsible and accountable for your progress will help you get past sticking points.

Step three

Involve senior management in the process and make sure they get regular and transparent updates on the project. If they don't buy in, any efforts will fail. I have found it helpful to clearly dictate general rules or guidelines for experimental stuff, which helps keep management and developers aligned: management knows what to expect, and developers know how to stay on track.

Step four

Assemble your team. One way to find the right talent is to develop your own, which I discussed in an earlier chapter. Another way is to start looking for people whose skillsets match your needs. Currently, most PhD students, graduates, and other AI talent are flocking to the big tech companies and research shops, but that won't last. In the meantime, there are other ways of finding a good team.

Outsource your AI needs and hire a vendor. This may be the simplest approach. It may also allow you to pursue multiple solutions in a shorter period of time.

Partner with a fintech that needs access to the data. One of my favorite approaches has been to offer data and a pilot in exchange for warrants in the fintech. Partnerships are a good way to build symbiotic relationships that ensure mutual success.

Provide broad AI training in-house and democratize the process. Bring in new experts monthly to speak about or train people on specific issues. Make sure everyone in the organizations sees and understands what direction you're heading.

Regardless of which approach you take toward bringing in the right people, don't forget your non-AI staff. Their buy-in could make or break your project. Even though they're not working on the project, they might still be able to help (or hurt) your goal.

If you do have the resources to hire a talented AI engineer or two, congratulations! You're ahead of the game. Just remember not to bog them down with tedious IT work. Putting them on regular IT duty will bury your AI project and contribute to high levels of job dissatisfaction in your AI team.

What Should My AI Team Look Like?

Depending on the size of your financial institution, your team might be only one person, or it could be many. Any team has members with specific strengths, and it's important to make sure that your team members can fill a few key roles.

Business Owner/Translator: This person is responsible for communication among or across business units. They should prioritize requests and opportunities.

Data Scientist/Engineers: This role develops use cases for business units. Much of their effort goes toward developing algorithms and analyzing data.

Visualization Analyst: Your visualization analyst develops dashboards and reports for business unit owners. This role helps people understand exactly what the AI is accomplishing.

Workflow Integrator: The role of the workflow integrator is to find integration pathways into various business units. They may create prototypes and help develop use cases.

Delivery Manager: The delivery manager determines whether use cases or prototypes solve the problems that they're supposed to solve. Ultimately, they make sure a project delivers the desired results.

Budgeting for AI

Knowing how to budget for AI is a very tough problem for financial institutions. For smaller organizations, off-the-shelf software and partners are the best bet. Another option is to partner with similar organizations in different markets so you can help each other without competing.

For larger institutions, you might want to see some top opportunities (outlined below) and calculate the potential impact of success. Then, create a funding calculation that you can measure against.

For example:

Project/Effort	ROI	Likelihood of Success
Call Center	$1m	75%
Chatbot	$400k	30%
Loan Underwriting	$600k	90%
Contract Review	$200k	100%

It doesn't matter whether the total value is $200k, $2m, or $200m. Simply take a percentage of the likely weighted sum and allocate a percentage of that budget. It probably won't be right, but it will establish some early KPIs that will allow you to evaluate and determine success in a quantitative approach.

Getting Buy-In

Your strategy for getting buy-in might differ depending on your position in your financial institution. If you're the president or CEO, you might have more clout. If you're in management, getting your C-level team on board might take more work.

I have a few ideas about how to get buy-in, but none of them are a silver bullet. Still, it's worth trying any of these strategies. **Try these strategies to convince your bosses to begin working with AI:**

Have them read this book. It might help them see the reality of AI in the financial industry.

Show them AI in action, especially if another financial institution is using it. It may help to illustrate how AI is both attainable and, if ignored, a potential existential threat.

Bring them a project proposal. It's easy to dismiss vague ideas, but it's a lot harder to dismiss a good plan.

Discuss the bottom line. AI is a long-term investment, and it will pay off. If you can clearly illustrate it, you've got a winning strategy.

These are just a few ideas, and if you have your own way of getting C-level buy-in, then you probably know best. As with most things in this book, I defer to your creativity and expertise. Just remember: getting C-level buy-in is great, but it's only the first step. The next step is getting buy-in from the rest of your organization.

If you are a C-level executive, getting buy-in is a bit different. You get to skip right ahead to convincing the rest of your institution to believe in your science fiction adventure. (Of course, framing AI projects in that way—as sci-fi adventures—sounds totally cool, but it's also unproductive.) This is an area where, and I cannot stress this enough, you have to make it very obvious that AI is not just possible—it's already here, your competitors are using it, and it's attainable even for the smallest financial institutions.

Some potential ways of getting buy-in from the rest of your staff may include:

Have them read this book. I cover a lot of basics in here.

Show them some of the AI that has already hit the financial market. Get them excited about the possibilities.

Hold a meeting to discuss common pain points. See what kinds of AI solutions might address those pain points. Showing people how AI can help solve their problems or make their lives easier is a good way to build excitement and demand.

Invite more people to participate or contribute to your AI project. There are few better ways to facilitate buy-in than letting people feel ownership in or responsibility for some of the action.

Again, you may have better ideas. And, depending on your position and your institutional climate, you may have to build this excitement incrementally instead of all at once. That's okay. It's better to start that part of the journey early. Don't put it off because it's hard! That's a surefire way of never getting anything done.

16

CONCLUSION

I will be the first to admit that I jump to conclusions quickly. The path here is obvious to me.

First, the fintech industry is growing at faster than 1,000 fintechs per year. Traditional banks and credit unions are shrinking by over 500. Eventually, there will be more fintechs than banks and credit unions. And eventually, they will also consolidate. Fintech consolidation could have major existential implications for the future of all financial institutions. Imagine an investment platform with a high-yield savings account, a checking account, a loan platform, and more. It could have all the services of a traditional financial institution, but with access to far more technology and a much smaller overhead.

Second, 90% of all fintechs I come across are using AI in their products. All of them are built on the cloud, because the cloud features robust and easy-to-use AI tools and low capital costs. AI requires a tantalizing admixture of technology and culture. Both require effort to update.

Third, very few credit unions and banks are truly leveraging the cloud. They are stuck in their slow, entrenched infrastructures. They're waiting to be dragged kicking and screaming into modernity without realizing that things like the cloud are considered mundane at this point. The longer they wait to A) get on the cloud, B) leverage analytics, and C) leverage cloud-based AI tools, the bigger the gap between the traditional players and the fintechs will grow. If we wait long enough, the fintechs will have such a huge advantage that the banks and credit unions won't be able to change fast enough. The years of head starts that fintechs have had will have put them light years ahead—banks and credit unions won't be able to catch up at all.

> Think Polaroid vs. Digital photography. There was no amount of improved chemical photographic development that could compete with the pace at which digital photography was improving. This is the stuff that vanquishes industries.

At present, our AI technology is creeping up on mastery of ANI while making steady progress toward AGI. It is likely that within the next decade or two, we will have essentially perfected ANI, and tools like machine learning and NLP will as problem-free and ubiquitous as smartphones are now. Perhaps a decade after that, and we may be looking at AGI. Getting beyond AGI could still be 20–100 years away, but that's well within many of our lifetimes. Regardless of when SAI occurs, even just the developments in ANI and the emergence of AGI will have revolutionary implications.

I know I keep talking about how AI is already here and that it has been around for years now. Fortunately, it's not too late to get in the game yet. Sure, you may be a bit behind in the AI race, and so it'll be harder to establish yourself as an innovator with key differentiators now. But we're still in the early stages of working with AI. This is the beginning of a new era, and credit unions and banks that work with AI now will have a huge advantage as the technology matures. Fintechs may be ahead on technology, but traditional financial institutions have a marked advantage with more customers, members, data, and brand recognition. That's a lot of leverage with which to capture emerging markets.

So far in my time on the planet, I have seen the rise of the mainframe, the desktop computer, the internet, smartphones, the cloud, and even wearable tech that surpasses the computing power of the supercomputers that my grandfather used to build. At this point, I can smell the emergence of the next major step up— the next section of the technological S-curve. That next step is artificial intelligence.

I have seen each wave of technology come, blindside those who didn't pay attention, and allow forward-thinking people to ride that wave like pros. Technological waves, like ocean waves, are unforgiving. But if they can be harnessed properly, they can get us where we're going—and fast.

The question for you is, what do you want to do with AI? You have the market at your fingertips. And the technology is just within reach. The industry is prime for change, growth, and disruption. It may not be too late now, but with the accelerating speed of technological change, that may not be true for long. It's time to choose your own adventure. Just remember: fortune favors the bold.

Good luck.

APPENDIX

NATURAL LANGUAGE PROCESSING AND MACHINE LEARNING

I discuss several emerging technologies throughout the book. These technologies form the backbone of current AI applications and use cases. If you're looking for further clarification about some of the tools that people are using today, then this section is a good starting place.

I'll try to keep it very general—the internet is already full of detailed, highly-technical explanations of how these technologies work. This section will just be a general overview of a couple basic aspects of AI. If you're already an expert, you could probably skip this appendix altogether. However, if you're not an expert, this appendix could be critical to understanding the rest of the book.

Machine Learning

Machine learning is currently one of the basic building blocks of AI technology. Machine learning is a type of algorithm that can modify and improve itself to optimize performance on particular tasks. As the algorithm—or "model"—gains more experience and works with more data, it refines itself as it "learns."

Humans give machine learning algorithms a goal and certain parameters. For example, with Deep Blue, humans defined some goals: find the best move available, don't allow the opponent to checkmate the king, and checkmate the opposing king. The parameters include things like: the moves must be legal, openings and defenses should be rooted in theory, and computing power and time may be limited against human opponents.

With those goals and parameters, the algorithm goes to work, playing thousands or millions of games against itself to learn. Many of the early steps result in absolute blunders. Fortunately, those early steps take a remarkably short amount of time (think seconds, minutes, or hours). Machine learning algorithms quickly learn which moves are bad, and they stop making those moves (and any moves like them). Instead, they look for legal options within their parameters that help them better accomplish their goals, quickly discarding any moves or strategies that might hinder success.

Chess is merely a convenient example, though. In reality, there are many more applications for machine learning than just reinventing the Mechanical Turk. Machine learning helps to detect spam, file legal paperwork, read the writing on checks, find patterns in mountains of data, make predictions, and more.

One form of machine learning—deep learning—can crunch enormous quantities of complex data and turn it into various outputs: winning strategies in strategy games with imperfect knowledge (such as poker and *StarCraft II*), financial trading, and image recognition and generation.

If you've ever been impressed by Netflix or Spotify's recommendations, or if you've ever seen an ad on your phone that directly referenced a product you were talking about the day before, then you can thank (or blame) machine learning accordingly. But that's not all! Machine learning powers weather forecasting, your digital assistant (Siri, Alexa, etc.), and search engines.

But not all machine learning works the same way. Most machine learning methods fit into one of two categories: supervised and unsupervised learning.

Supervised Machine Learning

Supervised machine learning focuses on targeted or specific outcomes (for example, which consumers are likely to be delinquent on a loan payment). The algorithm is trained by researchers who provide data, analyze the result, and then highlight the most desired outcome, which teaches the algorithm which results are good.

The hands-on approach with the data, the models, and showing the computer what kinds of outcomes are most desirable mean that human researchers or operators are essentially handholding or babysitting their algorithms. That's why it's called "supervised" machine learning.

As the model works with more data, more desired results appear, and researchers continue highlighting the best outcomes to refine their product. Over time, the model is able to make correlations or predictions that far exceed what traditional computers or expert humans could hope to accomplish.

Unsupervised Machine Learning

Unsupervised machine learning is a little different from supervised machine learning. With supervised models, researchers know what kind of outputs they want, and they train their algorithms to most faithfully deliver their desired outputs. The goal of unsupervised learning is to detect patterns, groupings, probabilities, clusters, and density estimations in data. It doesn't seek a predefined answer—it seeks to group data into its underlying structures.

There are several different unsupervised machine learning model types out there, but they're less common than supervised models at the moment. In the financial industry, most unsupervised machine learning is used to assess member profitability segments in the traditional A–E approach. "A" members are the most profitable and loyal, whereas "E" members are cherry pickers who chase price and rate, but are unlikely to be profitable.

Reinforcement Learning

Reinforcement learning is a little different from both structured and unstructured learning. Reinforcement learning helps computers and operators determine the ideal behavior or outcome given a goal and a set of data. Generally, reinforcement machine learning models are used to make specific decisions.

Credit modeling is a good example of reinforcement machine learning. Banks and credit unions provide data aimed at understanding which consumers will repay their debts and how much debt they can absorb. Then, they use reinforcement machine learning models to evaluate and make decisions about loan approval.

It's All Machine Learning, Though

Although there are three different types of machine learning, they all thrive on data. The more data they have, the better their ability to make predictions, decisions, and detect patterns. Banks and credit unions generate incredible quantities of data daily through transactions and engagement. That means the financial industry holds huge opportunities for key insights, service improvements, and capabilities based on the volumes of data produced daily.

Still, machine learning isn't the only prominent aspect of AI that tech-oriented industries feature prominently. Another aspect of AI is the backbone of virtual assistants, chatbots, and other human–computer interfaces.

Natural Language Processing

NLP is a field concerns interactions between humans and computers. Some of the issues that NLP seeks to solve include speech and text recognition, language understanding, language generation, and translation. Computers look for patterns, context, and "meaning" in order to use it fluently. Siri, Cortana, Alexa, and fintechs like Posh and 30 Seconds to Fly rely in part on the ability for computers to understand human communication.

Easier said than done, of course.

Normal conversations between people aren't always linear. You might be asking your kid to take out the trash when you get interrupted by your wife, who wants you to make a pot of coffee. Your ability to follow two conversations and sets of requests is actually an impressive feat. Some NLP programs still have difficulty following conversational threads, and they respond only to the most immediate input. That fading tendency led me to one of my favorite jokes in protest chant form:

Human: What do we want?

Computer: Natural language processing!

Human: When do we want it?

Computer: When do we want what?

Early NLP was definitely less impressive than it is today. If you ever reached a call center and talked to the voice recognition system, only to repeat yourself over and over no avail, then you know how bad it was. Well, those days are over. AI like Alexa, Google Home, Siri, and other voice and chatbots are evolving rapidly for better listening and conversing.

Natural Language Interaction (NLI)

Natural language interaction falls under the greater NLP umbrella. NLI is geared toward making computers more human-like in the way they interact. Humans use complex sentences and don't always speak or write linearly. Consequently, NLI helps machines follow difficult linguistic habits, like sentences that contain several bits of important information.

Natural Language Generation (NLG)

As I write this, I have an idea what I want to say. Yet, there are so many different ways to say things. Which word do I choose first? When do I introduce my subject or my predicate? Which other words should I write so it all makes sense? How do I order them?

Whereas NLI focuses on how to interact with language, NLG is focused on how to produce it. When computers write or speak, they use NLG to form their sentences. If they didn't, they'd just jam a bunch of words together and hope for the best.

Natural Language Understanding (NLU)

Natural language understanding is the next step in NLP evolution. The purpose of NLU is to understand nuance and context by analyzing how language is usually used.

Aided by NLU, a few NLP algorithms have shown some eerie results: in 2018, Alibaba's NLP AI outperformed even the most literate humans in a Stanford University reading comprehension test. Then, in 2019, researchers at OpenAI decided not to release a fully-functional language-generation program because it was able to write credibly well in a multitude of styles. They were worried about its potential to generate credible news stories or otherwise mislead humans for malicious intent.

It's All Natural Language Processing, Though

If you need more proof that NLP is far better than it was previously, try this on for size: in mid-2018, Google announced and demonstrated its AI Natural Processing assistant call a restaurant to make a reservation. The human on the other end had no idea that they were speaking with a computer.

For many of us, that sounds scary (in an annoying sort of way). You might worry that the all-too-frequent spam calls these days will get more sophisticated. If computers can sound like humans, you might ask:

Is this caller human?

How can I detect fraud or authenticate end users?

When AI assistants call your call center will you fulfill their requests?

Machine Learning Platforms

In my time interviewing various companies for this book, they all used the same three platforms. While there may be others out there, these three have shown to be the most common and the most accessible. However, if one of these platforms isn't right for your financial institution, then it wouldn't be hard to find something that better fits your needs.

Tensorflow

Tensorflow is Google's open-sourced AI engine. Its open source format sets it apart from Amazon's and Mircosoft's offerings by democratizing their approach. The idea is that a rising tide lifts all ships— the more people that use the platform, the more resources there are for everyone.

Google provides Tensorflow to organizations for use in classification, perception, understanding, discovering, prediction, and creation. In general, this is a great example of the early commercialization of machine learning and artificial intelligence.

Amazon Web Services AI Toolkit

The Amazon Web Services (AWS) cloud enables easy use of Amazon's AI toolkit. Amazon offers Amazon Machine Learning and Amazon Sagemaker to organizations who need a stable, high-quality AI platform. The only drawback of Amazon is that currently, they don't support unsupervised learning.

Sagemaker is Amazon's platform for data scientists. With Sagemaker, you just upload data and begin using the extensive library of tools, including things like regression analysis, image classification, natural language processing, and many of the other examples discussed in this book.

Microsoft AI Tools

Microsoft is also strong in the AI platform arena. They offer two services. The first service they offer is their Machine Learning Studio (ML Studio), which allows a simple graphical drag and drop environment in a workflow style environment. Their ML Studio supports over 100 different machine learning models, providing a flexible array of possibilities for almost any application. The other service is the bot service. This service uses more API-driven learning.

Several of the companies in this book use or have used Microsoft's AI tools with varying degrees of success. It's very intuitive, so it's an easy platform on which to experiment.

Machine Learning Uses

Most people use machine learning for at least one of the following five use cases:

- Voice and sound recognition
- Text-based applications
- Image recognition
- Time series (recommendations)
- Video detection

Almost every industry can use at least one of those features, and it's easy to see why. Let's look at a typical financial institution.

Voice recognition can assist or replace call centers. Want to know who is calling? How they are feeling? What their concerns are? AI can help with that, reducing the amount of work your people have to do.

Text-based applications can help with chat and statement history. Want to help people better understand their transactions? Want to help them set up bill pay? Text-based applications can do that.

Image recognition reads checks and documents. Beyond just reading bad handwriting, image recognition could help with fraud detection, see that documents are signed correctly, and ensure that the right documents are being used in any scenario.

Time series can help with recommendations. If you want to show members how other people use different services, you could accelerate product adoption. (Netflix's movie recommendations are an example of this in action.)

Video detection can assist with fraud detection. Tying credit union ATM cameras, branch cameras, etc. into a centralized analysis system could potentially spot fraud as it occurs, or it could identify transactions that indicate a higher likelihood of fraud, because the AI would be able to visually authenticate identity.

Those are just five examples of how a machine ecosystem can begin transforming your institution. To prepare for that kind of change, you would need to focus on getting your data normalized, prioritized, and anonymized so that it doesn't have personally identifiably information (PII). That kind of preparation should be a big priority if you want to take advantage of some easy machine learning wins.

Machine Learning APIs

Of the platforms listed above—Tensorflow, AWS, and Microsoft AI, all three offer APIs that allow for a variety off-the-shelf processing and machine learning tools. These include:

Speech and text processing

Image analysis and comparison

Video analysis and comparison

Each of these areas has about 25 different differentiating variables or features. Banks and credit unions should begin using these mature toolsets immediately, but strategically. Figure out what will work best for you, and then zero in on which platform will provide you the best opportunity to achieve your goals. It's important to keep in mind which platforms offer the kind of APIs that you'll need to undertake your best AI-based projects.

Structured and Unstructured Data Models

Yes, there are inconceivable amounts of data out there. And no, they're not all the same. The structure of the data is one easy way to distinguish the two.

Structured Data

Structured data is data for which all quantities are known (e.g. quantitative data). Structured data fits neatly into forms, fields, spreadsheets, graphs, and other simple ways of storing information. Structured data includes things like names, dates, transaction histories, credit scores, addresses, etc. Basically, if the data seems like a fact of some sort, or if it can be put into a spreadsheet, it's probably structured data.

Structured data is very easy for machines to understand because values are either quantified or are easily quantifiable. Instead of figuring out what the data is, computers can determine what the data means. Structured data allows machine learning models to quickly understand the relationships between sets of data, leading to relatively simple, predictable outcomes. Fortunately, most traditional banking data is structured data.

Unstructured Data

Unstructured data is more ubiquitous, and it's much harder for machines to understand and work with. Examples of unstructured data include images, video, text, social media activity, and whatever data our smart home devices generate. Essentially, any data that doesn't fit neatly into traditional transaction and financial data falls in this category.

As bankers and STEM graduates, many of us are not known for our creativity or our understanding of the unstructured world. By definition, our regulated worlds want to neatly organize data and have our deposits, loans, consumers put into neat little boxes. This is an area where machine learning is making major strides: it can recognize images and handwritten text, find patterns in web browsing history and site interaction, and follow trends in mobile app usage and other forms of digital engagement.

Unstructured data provides much of the fuel for predictive analytics at this point. Good analytics models need as much data as possible so that they can see the effects of every facet of a digital ecosystem, no matter how minor. Financial institutions could realize significant long-term competitive potential if they can collect and leverage unstructured data.